Navigating Seasons of Change

Dr. James S. McIntyre, Sr.

Navigating Seasons of Change

Dr. James S. McIntyre, Sr.

NVP

NUVISION PUBLISHING

NAVIGATING SEASONS OF
CHANGE

DR. JAMES S. MCINTYRE, SR.

FOREWORD BY PRESIDING BISHOP TIM HILL

PRAISE FOR
Navigating Seasons of Change

It's been called the "C" word—*change*—everybody needs it, but no one wants to go first.

Repentance yields a changed heart. This is deeper than *remorse,* which could include tears of regret, but no true change.

With a pastoral calling to guide others in knowing the life-changing power of Jesus Christ, Dr. James S. McIntyre, Sr. gives practical and spiritual insights on how you can walk daily through change to be an overcomer—living a life that moves from glory to glory through the Spirit of the Lord.

-Dr. David E. Ramirez, D. Min.
Assistant General Overseer
Executive Director,
Division of Education
Church of God

"Change is one of the more contradictory terms in the English language, as it evokes a wide range of emotions, such as elation, fear, apprehension, and joy… just to name a few. James McIntyre has taken this complex word and broken it down into manageable parts to assist the believer in "navigating" it in a Spirit-led fashion."

-Bishop Gary Lewis
Secretary General
Church of God, Cleveland, TN

The task of directing, managing, and creating change is the primary task of an effective leader. In his book, *Navigating Seasons of Change,* my friend, James McIntyre, draws upon more than 20 years of leadership experience in ministry to help those who want healthy change in their lives and the organizations they are called to lead. This is a must-read for leaders who want to know how to bring about God's vision for themselves and the ministries they lead.

-Dr. Michael D. Reynolds,
Director of Ministerial Development,
Church of God (Cleveland, TN)

Dr. James S. McIntyre has written a must-read book to assist pastors and leaders in navigating ministry in changing times. *Navigating Seasons of Change* challenges pastors to learn the art of connectivity, while embracing and conquering the frustrations of change. Dr. McIntyre believes that failing to embrace change will lead to aimless navigation in leadership. He contends that leadership must embrace change or risk losing direction. When leaders acquire these navigational skills, they understand how to empower those whom they lead to learn the art of productivity while casting a vision to succeed. Navigating Seasons of Change will inform, empower, and motivate leaders who are striving for the next level of ministry.

-Bishop Dr. Kenneth L. Hill, D. Div.
Administrative Bishop
Executive Council Member
Church of God, Cleveland, TN

Dr. James McIntyre's book, *Navigating the Seasons of Change,* is a timely and invaluable resource for anyone grappling with the inevitability of change. In a world where change is constant, Dr. McIntyre offers profound insights and practical wisdom on how to not only survive but thrive amidst the ebb and flow of life's transitions. With clarity and empathy, Dr. McIntyre acknowledges the inherent challenges and frustrations that accompany change. Yet, he empowers readers to embrace change as an opportunity for growth and transformation. By emphasizing the importance of intentionality and personal responsibility, he guides readers through a journey of self-discovery and empowerment. What sets *Navigating the Seasons of Change* apart is Dr. McIntyre's unique approach to navigating change. Through the framework of the "five Ps" for change and thought-provoking questions, he provides readers with a blueprint for making informed decisions and navigating the complexities of change with confidence and resilience. Whether you're facing a career transition, a relationship change, or simply navigating the ups and downs of life, this book offers invaluable guidance and inspiration. Dr. McIntyre's expertise and compassionate voice shines through every page, making *Navigating the Seasons of Change* a must-read for anyone seeking to navigate life's inevitable transitions with grace and purpose.

-Derwood L. Perkins, PhD
Administrative Bishop, Mississippi

It is said that nothing is constant like change. The world is changing at an even greater pace as technology, globalization, demographic shifts and environmental issues play an even more prominent role in our lives. On a recent trip to London, I sat intrigued as a robotic janitor swept the aisle while announcing to those walking by to use caution. Change is taking place right around us and our failure to respond appropriately undermines any chance for future impact. The prominent philosopher Alvin Toffler once stated, "The illiterate of the 21st century will not be those who cannot read and write, but those who cannot learn, unlearn and relearn." We are living in the days when the cycle for relearning loops quicker and quicker. Since the Church of Jesus Christ does not exist in a vacuum, it stands to reason that the surrounding changes will have a corresponding impact on the functioning of the body of Christ. While our message remains the same, our methodology must respond to the times. While the centuries of monastic communities helped to spread Christianity afar, Christ promoted the metaphor of salt and light to demonstrate that our witness as believers require engagement with a corrupt and immoral world. Dr. James McIntyre has courageously taken on the task of speaking to this relevant issue in his book, *Navigating Seasons of Change.* He speaks with the heart of a pastor to pastors and ministry-leaders, that we do not have the luxury of avoiding the changes around us, but instead commissioned by our Lord to boldly challenge and navigate the shifting movements. I am encouraged by the fact that my dear friend did not only identify the changes but also offered solid and relevant suggestions to help on the journey. This book is a must-read for modern day ministry leaders at all levels of ministry.

-Bishop R. C. Hugh Nelson
Executive Council Member
Senior Pastor of Ebenezer Urban Ministry Center

Unless otherwise noted, all Scripture quotations are taken from the NKJV, the New King James Version, Copyright © 1979, 1980, 1982, 1990, 1995, Thomas Nelson Inc., Publishers. All rights reserved.

Scripture quotations marked KJV are taken from the King James Version of the Holy Bible, now in Public Domain.

Scripture quotations marked NIV are taken from the Holy Bible, New International Version®. NIV®. Copyright © 1973, 1978, 1984, 2011 by Biblica, Inc.®. Used by permission. All rights reserved.

Scripture quotations marked NASB are taken from the New American Standard Bible®. Copyright © 1960, 1971, 1977, 1995, 2020 by The Lockman Foundation. All rights reserved.

Scripture quotations marked KJ21 are taken from the 21st-Century King James Version. Copyright © 1994 by Deuel Enterprises, Inc.

Scripture quotations marked MSG are taken from The Message. Copyright © 1993, 2002, 2018 by Eugene H. Peterson.

Scripture quotations marked NLT are taken from the Holy Bible, New Living Translation, copyright © 1996, 2004, 2007. Used by permission of Tyndale House Publishers, Inc., Wheaton, Illinois 60189. All rights reserved.

Scripture quotations marked TLV are taken from the Tree of Life Version. Tree of Life (TLV) Translation of the Bible. Copyright © 2015 by The Messianic Jewish Family Bible Society.

ISBN#: 978-1-66640-884-3

Printed in the United States of America

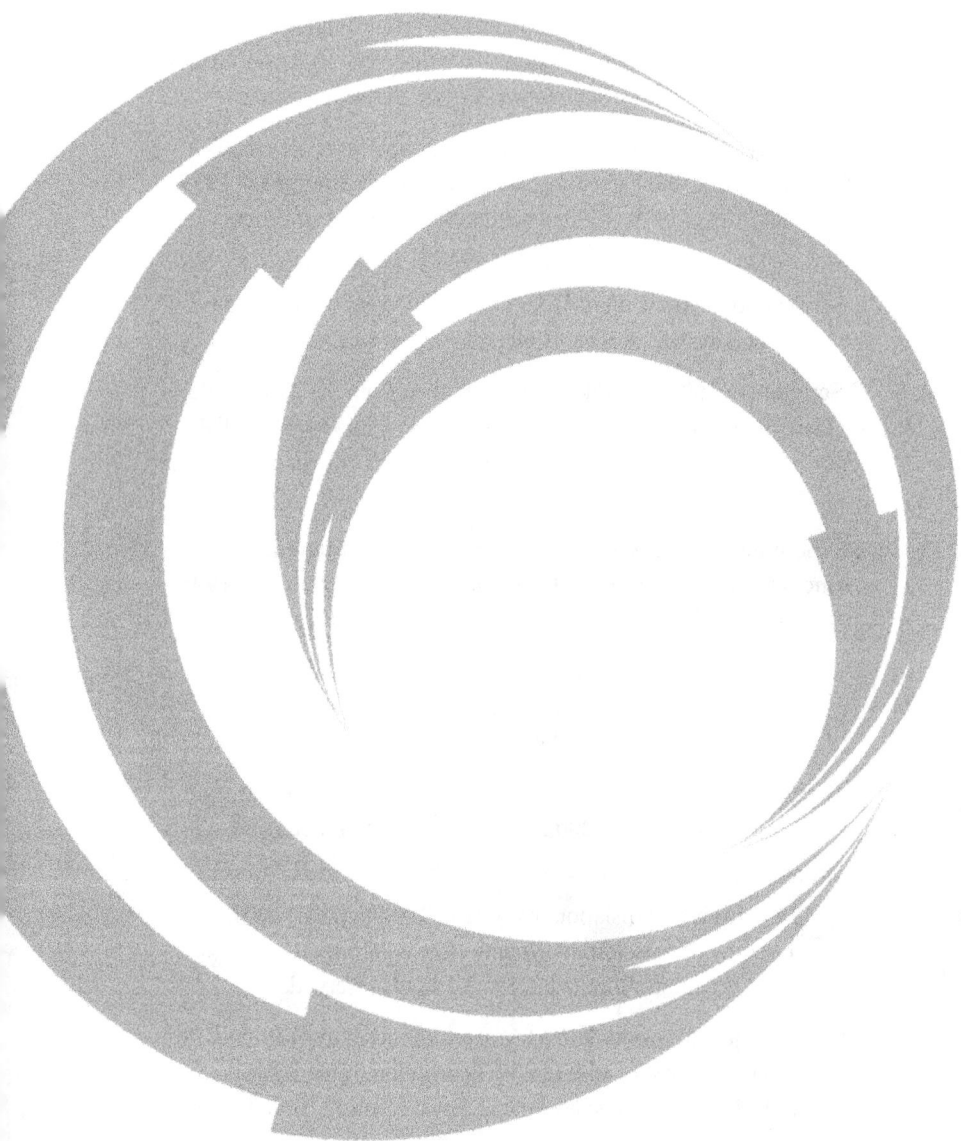

DEDICATION

To my lovely wife and life partner for over forty years, Lisa, who has seen me at my best and at my worst and still loves and respects me. I love you honey-thank you for sharing seasons of change with me.

To our three sons and daughter in love, James Jr., Jonathan, and Joshua and Sabre, whom I say as God said of His Son, Jesus; "I am well pleased."

To our beautiful grandchildren, Jayden Hunter, Jirah Sincere, Averie Grace, and James Douglas-
you are our joy.

To my precious mother Joyce Ann Wimbish, you are such a blessing to us, and we love you dearly.

To my siblings, Joyce and Glenn, Mike and Crystal, Sonya and Fred, and Casandra and Robert-
I love you all.

To our spiritual daughter, Adrianna Renee Reid who is a true blessing to our family.

CONTENTS

FOREWORD

Whether or not we admit it, no one likes change. Many people welcome a new challenge, whether through ministry, vocation, family, or even a positive health change. But if they are honest, the easier way to go is to continue to tread water, doing things as they have always been done. When change does come, it is often met with impatience, frustration, and disdain.

Dr. McIntyre's book is one of the most appropriately titled books out there. *Navigating Seasons of Change* speaks directly to helping get through those "seasons" that when taken literally, act out like the four seasons that come every year. Like clockwork, change behaves in the same manner as seasons: they will be here, before you, before you know it!

Despite its negativity, change can be channeled positively. While many times change cannot be prevented, it certainly does not have to be a dream killer. In this book, Dr. McIntyre examines the plethora of dynamics that come with change and presents it through a biblical lens and based on personal experience.

When it arrives, don't shun change, but embrace it. Realize that as God-fearing children of God we have the advantage in navigating through one of life's toughest dilemmas with the Savior on our side.

-Bishop Tim Hill
Presiding Bishop
Church of God,
Cleveland, Tennessee

ACKNOWLEDGMENTS

First and foremost, I honor God the Father, Christ our Redeemer, and the Holy Spirit, the Chief Administrator handling God's affairs here on the Earth. It is in and through them that all things are made possible. I acknowledge the following people who have made so many wonderful contributions in my life.

- My spiritual father, Bishop James C. Monroe Jr., whom I had the privilege of serving with for more than twenty years.
- To Dr. Timothy Hill, Presiding Bishop, and the International Executive Committee of the Church of God, who have honored me to serve in several international appointments in this great church—the Church of God.
- To several State Administrative Bishops who served the Eastern North Carolina region whom I have had the privilege of serving as the first elected State Council board member:
- Dennis Page, Dwight Spivey, and Wayne Brewer: Thank you for your mentorship and friendship.
- To Dr. Kenneth and Evangelist Janice Hill who have been role models and friends to Lisa and me for many, many years.
- To the members of the Cornerstone Family Worship Center COG, present and past—the only church that we were blessed to serve as pastor for more than twenty years. We love you dearly!
- To all whom I may not have mentioned here, but you have prayed and encouraged me to do this: "I sincerely thank you."

INTRODUCTION

This book has been designed to inspire, encourage, and challenge the reader to trust God in your seasons of change. He knows the plans He has for you. Just as He said to Jeremiah: "Before I formed you in the womb I knew you; Before you were born I sanctified you; I ordained you a prophet to the nations" (Jeremiah 1:5 NKJV). Nations are not just geographical regions around the world, but they are also the people whom you encounter throughout your life. So, regardless of whether you are in a classroom, on a football field, sitting behind a desk in an office, working in a factory, or serving in a ministry, you encounter people; therefore, you have the potential to become an **AGENT OF CHANGE** in their lives.

> While it is true that we can't plan or direct every aspect of our lives, it is also true that many of the decisions that we make have a profound outcome on who we are and what we will accomplish in life. The "Serenity Prayer" gives sound advice in this ever-changing world.

"God, grant me the serenity to
accept the things I cannot change,
the courage to change the things I can,
and the wisdom to know the difference."

Navigating seasons of change is one of the most important things you will ever do in your life.

I'm sure I don't have to tell you about how fast our world is changing, especially in more recent years. Over the last decade, we have witnessed our world navigate seasons of change through racial tensions, social and political upheaval, disastrous storms, and a global pandemic. We've gone from . . .

- Checkout clerks at the local Walmart to online shopping with curbside delivery.
- Driver-input navigating systems to self-drive vehicles.
- On-campus brick-and-mortar to online virtual classrooms.
- Predominantly in-person board meetings to hybrid on Zoom and other platforms.

All of which has made a devastating impact in our lives and on our world.

Then, there is the way we do church. The sad fact is that in an ever-changing, fast-paced global world, the church is, in many cases, lagging far behind with its means, methods, and sometimes even the message of reconciliation and redemption.

As a pastor, it didn't take me long to realize that if I wanted to be effective and relevant, then I had to be intentional about my responsibility to God, His mission, and the people He placed in my care. I quickly learned that as the leader I was charged with the ministry duty of setting the culture for the church. However, I must confess that it did not come easy. The truth is, there were several times when I made some "not-so-good" decisions that hurt the ministry. Thank the Lord, I learned from them and was able to rebound, which led to a successful pastorate at Cornerstone Family Worship Center Church of God in Washington, North Carolina.

It is my hope that after reading this book, you will be able to use some of the content I have shared to help you *navigate seasons of change* in your personal life, as well as the place and people you are privileged to serve.

THIS WEEK

W

TH

Sharpie. Pen.

CHAPTER 1
CHANGE

From the time we take our first breath as a baby coming into the world, until that day when breath leaves our body, we will be in the process of life known as change. We live in a world where everything around us is experiencing constant change. Every day brings with it something new, daring, exciting, and yes, even scary at times. All around us, things are constantly moving—many times, at a rapid pace. Seemingly, it is all one can do to try to keep up with everything happening around us. Some changes are positive while others may be negative. Some are good and some are not so good. Some we like; others we disdain. Some we have control over, others we do not. While it may be true that we cannot control some of the changes, we can certainly navigate through them.

Like a compass in the hand of an explorer, we can navigate through the murky challenges of change in our lives and our ministry assignments with the mindset to grow and experience the best life instead of merely existing. The Lord has provided the compass in the person of the Holy Spirit. It is He who comes alongside us to lead, guide, and comfort us as we manage the day-to-day affairs of life and ministry.

Every day we make the decision to change something about ourselves or something that may have an effect on or around us. These decisions can either

> "If we don't change, we don't grow. If we don't grow, we aren't really living."
> ------- Gail Sheehy

propel us into great benefits or they can reduce us to sorrow and regret. We must face the fact: Change is here to stay, whether we like it or not. So, the best thing we can do is try our best to navigate the ever winding and twisting curves in this world of change. There is hope for us who serve the Lord. We are admonished and encouraged to know that we do not have to travel this ever-changing life without help. The Word of God instructs us to, *"Acknowledge Him in all [our] ways and He will direct [our] paths."* (See Proverbs 3:6). Yes, even in a fast-paced ever-changing world we have the Lord's ever abiding assurance and assistance. However, we are still responsible for making decisions for change. Whether it is because of something we have done, or something that is not our fault, it still requires a decision to be made in one way or another. When that happens, three keys should be considered:

The keys to change are…

1. *Acknowledge* the need for change. No matter where we find ourselves in this ever-changing world, we are in one of three stages. These three stages are true regardless of whatever job, profession, relationship, or ministry assignment in which we find ourselves. We must acknowledge the need to continue forward progress. To be fruitful and productive.

The first stage of life is called growth and productivity. This is not a difficult stage to acknowledge at all. As a matter of fact, it is one in which we all desire to be. The stage of growing, thriving, and increasingly moving forward makes us feel good. This stage of life speaks of living in the abundant blessings of God. Every one of us would like nothing better than to experience an increase in every facet of our lives, especially in this ever-changing world around us. The reality is, if we hope to continue growing, we must maintain a constant mindset to do everything in our power to move forward with the greatest of intentions. Even with our best efforts, there will always be something that will come to hinder or even stop the season of growth—that is called **CHANGE**. Life is not all peaches and cream. Sometimes, there will be thorns and thistles. It is important that we recognize and acknowledge that, because the moment we don't recognize or acknowledge it, we enter life stage two. This is a very critical stage in life. This second stage comes to stagnation or plateau, which causes no growth or productivity.

The second stage in life is called plateau. This is known as the place of standstill, stagnation, or comfort zone. This is a dangerous stage because growth has stopped. Nothing is happening; nothing is moving.

Again, these are stages of life that will be experienced in our personal lives, in relationships, careers, and yes, even in our ministry assignment. If we are not growing and producing, then we are stagnated and nonproductive. There can be many reasons that contribute to this. Call it what it is—**SEASONS OF CHANGE.** Something has happened. In relationships, it could be because of taking each other for granted. In a profession, it could be the willingness not to keep up with current personal or market trends. In ministry, it could be the failure to acknowledge the need to change from the way we always did things. It may even be contributed to the fear of the unknown or the unwillingness to try something new. Maybe it is a lack of knowledge or the feeling of failing. Maybe it's the problem of getting others to take ownership of the vision. Whatever it may be, the reality is that change has happened and now productivity is lost. Sadly, that is the state of many of the ministries today. If something is not done to change this situation, the final stage of life is evident.

The final stage in this world of change is the most critical, and if something is not done quickly all will be lost. This is the stage where you cease to exist—death is a surety. To put it bluntly, it is the stage of decline or death. Have I gotten your attention? When things plateau, if something does not happen quickly to get moving forward again, then the process changes from growth to stagnation, and finally death will surely happen. Many times, it is not a matter of how, but when. The good news is that death does not have to take place. If you act fast, change can happen and growth can be experienced again. Acknowledge what stage you are in and make the necessary adjustments. This brings me to my next step in the change process—*acceptance.*

2. *Accept* is to come to grips with the reality of where you are and that there is a need for another type of change. It means taking the

> "To improve is to change; to be perfect is to change often."
> — Winston Churchill

responsibility and owning up to where you are in the process. To accept is to not make excuses but to roll up your sleeves, get in the trenches, and go to work. It doesn't matter if it's a relationship, a professional, personal, or ministry problem, especially if you are the leader. I mentioned earlier that the leader is responsible for setting the culture. You have to be willing to put in the work to turn things around. I'm not going to tell you that it will be easy. But what I will say is—you have all you need to get it done, and what you don't have, God can provide it for you. You can do it! The final level in the change process is called *adapt.*

3. *Adapt* means to make decisions to change directions and embrace the new path that will set you on the course of growth and productivity again. I will talk more about this in later chapters. What is most important is for you to understand that for new forward progress to take place, you may have to refine, retool, remodel, and yes, even release what is holding you back from the progress and product you desire. That could be old methods, that are sacred cows or traditions that may be hard to part with. It may even mean some people who can't or refuse to go with you or buy into where God is taking you.

One of the most difficult things to experience in the change process is releasing people. Difficult as it may be, the decision to move on and leave some behind must be made, especially if they are not willing to change for future growth. Believe me when I say, some people can't get past what we used to do or who we used to be. They are good people, but growth and productivity will necessitate getting the wrong people off the bus, getting the right people on the bus, and getting them in the right seats for future growth.

You have heard it said that God changes things, and He certainly can and does. God can do anything. However, I am more inclined than ever to believe that God changes people, and people change things. You see, people are who God chose to use on this earth to make things happen for His good pleasure. We who are His sons and daughters have been endowed with His Spirit which is at work in us to accomplish His will and bring glory to His name. When that happens, it is as if God himself were here on earth doing it.

Our prime example is His Son and our Savior Jesus Christ, whose entire life was used to do the will of His Father.

> ## Jesus' life was filled with defining moments of change.

From the time of His birth until He breathed His last breath here on this Earth. It all started with the exchange from His divine form into the natural form of humanity. From there, we follow the five major changes of His life in the New Testament Scriptures: (1) His Baptism in the Jordan; (2) His Transfiguration on the mountain; (3) His Crucifixion on Golgotha; (4) His Resurrection from the dead; and (5) His Ascension back to His rightful place, seated at the right side of the Father.

How comforting it is to know that in every life-changing situation, He remains focused on His purpose and assignment as given to Him by God. It did not matter how many times He experienced unbelief, rejection, criticism, slander, or any of the other life-changing circumstances that man experiences. He was committed to the cause, even to the point of death. Just as He did, so can we as well. He has become our high priest who indeed understands what we go through in this ever-changing, uncertain, and sometimes crazy world. I encourage you that in difficult times of change, go to Him and receive grace, mercy, and help in times of need. He is there waiting with open arms.

Hebrews 4:14-16 says: *"Seeing then that we have a great high priest, that is passed into the heavens, Jesus the Son of God, let us hold fast our profession. For we have not an high priest which cannot be touched with the feeling of our infirmities; but was in all points tempted like as we are, yet without sin. Let us therefore come boldly unto the throne of grace, that we may obtain mercy, and find grace to help in time of need"* (KJV).

What is change? "To make (someone or something) different; alter or modify." There are many synonyms for the word "change." Some of them are alteration, difference, modification, shift, variation, revision, revise, amendment.

If change is going to ever happen, it must start with you. Self-change is tough, but it's not impossible, nor does it have to be traumatic, according to change expert, Stan Goldberg, Ph.D. and author of *The 10 Rules of Change.* Change Is Frightening: We resist change, but fear of the unknown can result in clinging to status quo behaviors— no matter how bad they are. Change Requires Structure: Many people view structure as restrictive, something that inhibits spontaneity.

CHAPTER 2
DEFINING
MOMENTS OF
CHANGE

Defining moments of change happen when God directs your life in seasons that move you from one time span, one location, one task, or from one ministry assignment to another. These moments are marked by significant contributions from God that point back to the Lord ordering your footsteps. The Bible has several notable moments that mark seasons of change in individuals' lives.

Defining moments of change happen in our lives sometimes when we don't know they are happening. These are times when God himself in the counsel of His own will, determining that change is needed. I know we sometimes think we are in control of our destiny; therefore, we make choices that have an impact on and in our lives. The reality is, if God doesn't breathe on our plans and decisions, nothing happens. God's Word instructs us to always acknowledge Him in all our ways, and He will direct our paths (see Proverbs 3:6).

In every decision, choice, or path we take, we must seek God for His divine will, not His permissive will for our lives. Divine because He knows what is best for us. As the Lord said through the prophet Jeremiah: *"For I know the thoughts that I think toward you, saith the LORD, thoughts of peace, and not of evil, to give you an expected end"*(Jeremiah 29:11 KJV). May I submit to you, God's thoughts are far better than ours. He knows what is best for us and what we need. All we have to do is simply trust Him and do as His Word instructs us in Proverbs. *"In all thy ways acknowledge him, and he shall direct thy paths"* (Proverbs 3:6).

Defining moments of change make times significant when the impossible was inevitable.

Many times, in the life of Jesus, we see that in the lives of those He encountered. For example, the woman with the issue of blood. After twelve long years of suffering, segregation, and seclusion, she heard that Jesus was coming to her town, on His way to Jarius' house, where he had a twelve-year-old daughter lying sick. On this particular morning, this woman woke up because of the noise outside her home (paraphrasing). As this crowd passes her house, she hears someone say, Jesus the healer is in town. She probably thought within herself, today is the day for things to change. She probably said, "I've been to doctor after doctor, spent all my money, and instead of getting better, I've gotten worse." At least that's what the Bible says. (It had to come from her because no one knew her story better than she did.)

On this morning, she decided to get herself together and get in the crowd of people pressing past her house. On this day, she's not concerned with the Jewish legalism that says she is unclean and shouldn't be touching or even be around people. She is desperate, and desperate situations require desperate measures. Today will be her day to receive the healing miracle that she so desired. Her defining moment of change is right in her eyesight, right at arm's length. So, she stooped down, and inconspicuously reached around one of the disciples and touched the hem of Jesus' garment. **The response was instantaneous—she experienced her defining moment of change.** Her hemorrhaging stopped. Immediately, the procession stopped. Jesus turned around and asked the question, "Who touched me?" To that, one of the disciples replied, all these people around You, bumping into You, and You ask, who touched You? To that, Jesus replied, this was an unusual touch. To that I might add, everyone bumping into Jesus is not touching Him. Only those who move by faith for that which seems impossible. Now, this is my story, so let me tell it the way I see it!

Jesus proceeded to say, this was not an ordinary touch. This touch pulled something (virtue) out of Me. Virtue here is defined by Webster as: "The radical sense of strength, from straining, stretching, extending." When Jesus said virtue has gone out of me, He is literally saying radical strength has left me. Now here is the crazy thing about it, the woman never touched His flesh, only the garment He was wearing. That garment had enough power in it to dry up this woman's "issue of blood." After she could no longer hide, she ran to Jesus, knelt down at his feet and told Him her condition and her purpose for touching Him. To that, Jesus replied: *"Daughter, be of good comfort: thy faith hath made thee whole; go in peace"* (Luke 8:48 KJV). What this woman received that day far surpassed just her healing. Jesus proclaimed that she was made whole. In other words, to be healed, spoke of just her physical condition. However, to "be made whole," spoke of not only the physical condition, but also her mental, emotional, psychological, relational, and economic situations. That day she experienced a complete change. *This was her defining moment of change.*

Now, back to Jairus, who must have been feeling desperate. You know how you feel when someone jumps in front of you in the supermarket line or someone cuts you off in traffic which causes you to get stopped by the traffic light. Yeah, that right there! I mean Jesus was on His way to his house to heal his little twelve-year-old daughter, and the woman out of nowhere interrupts Him. To make matters worse, the very next verse could have just sucked the life out of him. I mean he needed a defining moment of change fast.

Look at the very next verse: *"While he yet spake, there cometh one from the ruler of the synagogue's house, saying to him, Thy daughter is dead; trouble not the Master"* (Luke 8:49 KJV). Jairus' daughter was sick just a minute ago, but now she's dead. Look at how the man brings the news to him. "Your daughter is dead; stop worrying Jesus." There is nothing anyone can do. It's over. In fact, the professional mourners have already shown up at the house crying over the girl. Can you just imagine what's probably going through Jairus' mind? Maybe he's thinking, if Jesus had not stopped to help this lady, He would have made it on time and my daughter would still be alive. Maybe he's blaming Jesus for stopping. After all, He didn't have to stop, but He did. Jairus needed a miracle of a defining moment of change for him and his daughter.

So, look at what the miracle worker (Jesus) said in the next verse. Jesus said to Jairus and the crowd standing around; *"Fear not: believe only, and she shall be made whole"* (Luke 8:50 KJV). Jesus quickly took control of the situation by telling Jairus to be not afraid, but simply believe. In other words, have faith for your daughter's situation to change—not just change, but change for the better. He encouraged him by saying: "she shall be made whole!"

What Jesus didn't say was, Your daughter will be healed! He said, "Shall be made whole." You see, healing was automatic, but making her whole required a little more. Healing the little girl would simply bring her back to life. Making her whole would deal with all the emotional, physical, and mental issues that come along with what caused her to die in the first place. Jesus was saying, your daughter will be complete in every sense of the word.

Now there will be those who will want to prevent you from experiencing your "moments of change" miracles. Just as they were with Jesus and Jairus. You see them in the people who like to show up where there are dead things, because they can't see the miracle of living. So, the first thing Jesus had to do was kick out the professional mourners. Who, by the way, really didn't want to go. When they did leave, they laughed at Jesus and Jairus simply because they saw the situation as lifeless and dead. Jesus simply put all of them out.

Let me stop here and encourage you that there will be people who want nothing better than to hinder or block your "change moment." You must take the attitude of Jesus and **PUT THEM OUT!**

Not only did He put out the professional mourners, but He allowed only His inner circle—Peter, James, and John—along with the father and mother of the girl to come into the house with Him. Once in the house, Jesus steps to the bed and calls the young girl back to life and delivers her to her parents.

These are just a couple of examples of people who experienced moments of change in their lives. The Bible is full of them. Just to name a few: Blind Bartimaeus, widow of Nain, the man sitting at the Temple gates called "Beautiful," the man lying by the pool of Bethsaida, and the list goes on. What about Saul on the road to Damascus, or Pastor Peter who was chained between sixteen soldiers, and the apostle Paul when he was shipwrecked on the island of Malta—all of these experienced defining moments of change in their lives.

Not only has the Lord shown up and delivered these, but He has also done some pretty amazing things in my life, and yours as well. Just take a moment and think about how He showed up when the odds were stacked against you. Maybe you experienced a bad sickness, relationship problems, financial devastation, or a mental crisis. Whatever it was, God showed up and you are here to talk about how He gave you a defining moment of change and now your life is better.

CHAPTER 3
CHANGE IS DIFFICULT, BUT NECESSARY

In 2002, I assumed the role of pastor to the West 9th Street Church of God in Washington, North Carolina. This was the first church that I pastored. In fact, I followed a long-term pastor who had served there for more than 30 years. I remember saying these words to the church in my first meeting. "I wish I could tell you that all change is good. Quite to the contrary. While all change may not be good, the truth of the matter is that many times change is necessary. Change can be difficult, but if we're going to survive and do all that God put in my heart to do as the pastor of the church, it will require some changes."

You see, I was told when you are appointed to a church, do not go in and make any changes for at least a year. I completely ignored that. I made changes on the very first meeting, which, by the way, included some of the things they wanted to see changed. After some questions and feedback from them, I said, "We're going to have to make some changes; change may be difficult, but necessary if we're going to be successful in accomplishing the vision God put in our hearts for the church." These are some of the changes that were made that night. I changed the time of Sunday school from 10:00 a.m. to 9:30 a.m. Next, I changed the worship experience from 11:00 to 10:30 a.m. I changed the order of the morning worship experience, as well as the Wednesday night prayer service. I even changed how we would receive the tithes and offerings on Sunday morning. That was changed, because I was told that the church was receiving approximately six offerings on Sunday morning. Can you imagine, collecting six offerings? Thinking back now, I probably should have kept the six offerings. What we decided to do would be intentional: Receive one offering.

Changing from six offerings to one intentional way of worshiping in giving was received quite well. Especially since I said to them, "I will lead you in giving, and I'll never ask for anything I am not giving first." You see, one of the desires of the church was to build a new building. The current facility was small and seated approximately 130 people. The vision that God gave me earlier that day when I arrived in Washington was bigger than our current church. I learned quickly what it meant to be a visionary leader. I also quickly realized that if change was going to happen, it would have to be done with intentionality. It would not be enough to plan, strategize, set goals, and cast vision, if we were not going to exercise our faith, but also be committed to putting in the work.

During the early days of my pastorate, I focused on training leaders, developing systems, as well as ministries teams, while at the same time, casting a vision for a worship center and implementing various initiatives to help us achieve it. In addition to the crucial steps we took to train and develop our leaders, our priority was establishing a strong children's and youth ministry. We knew and understood that it was essential for the growth and survival of our future church. Through our efforts, our children's ministry grew rapidly, and we began experiencing exponential growth in our congregation. However, our success also presented some challenges. Within one year, we had already reached our maximum seating capacity, so we had to convert various spaces in the church to accommodate everyone. Our office became classrooms, and our fellowship hall and small kitchen were turned into a children's ministry area. Despite the challenges, we had an excellent team that ministered to the kids on their level, and we continued to work toward achieving the vision of new, larger facilities that we laid before the church.

Then, there was the challenge of seating for our Sunday worship experience. I remember seeing many times on a Sunday morning people turn around and leave because we had no place for them to sit in the sanctuary. The idea of having two services never entered my mind. I'm not sure why it didn't. All I can say is maybe it was because we were so focused on building a new church that would have classrooms, a fellowship hall, offices, and worship space to meet our growing church needs. I projected that it would take approximately five years before we would be able to purchase land and build such a facility. *What I thought would take place in five years, God miraculously blessed us to accomplish in two years.*

The church raised funds, and within the first year, we purchased property on the main highway coming into the city of Washington, NC. We bought about five acres of land on Highway 264, which included a nice home, and behind the house, was farmland. The owner of the property was, at that time, building a new home for himself and wanted to sell his current home, which was located on the property. He had heard that we were looking to purchase land for our new church. We met with him, looked at the house and land, and we felt the hand of God at work in the process.

The decision to purchase the land was met with our agreement to buy the house also. The owner said to us these words: "I'll sell you all the land you need to build your church if you buy my house too. At that time, the church was leasing a small home for me and my family, and the proposal to purchase the much larger home just seemed like the thing to do. So, we decided to purchase the home, with an additional lot next to it, along with a great portion of the farmland that was located behind both.

Now, the owner of the property had in his mind how much he wanted, and we had in our minds how much we wanted to give him for it. We began having conversations regarding the purchase of the home and property. At that time, the farmland behind the house was full of corn. We were told by the owner, If you purchase my home and this property, your people would never be hungry, they can eat all the corn they want. To that I replied that corn would have to go because we are going to put our church where it is planted—that corn is coming down. So, we began to discuss what we would pay for the property. We made him an offer of $150,000 for land and the nice house that sat on it. To that, he refused and made a counteroffer of $250,000. Of course, we rejected his offer. After several weeks of negotiating, we finally reached an agreeable settlement of $190,000. Within a few weeks, my family and I moved into the home, which was transitioned into the parsonage owned by the church. After staying in hotels, and a small rental home for what seemed like forever, we were ready for a larger space with more room. The land had several large trees on it. So, our first order of business was the removal of all the trees around the property that stood between the home and the land where the new church would be built. We hired a tree removal company who cut down all the trees, removed them from the land and graded the property, preparing it for our new worship center.

The Enemy Within:

Don't ever think that the enemy will sit quietly during your *season of navigating change.* The Bible gives us instruction to be watchful because our enemy, the devil, walks about seeking whom he may devour. He comes to steal your vision, kill your influence, and destroy your God- given plans and purpose. The sad fact is, it's not always someone from the outside; it's someone from the inside that can do the most harm.

During the early stages of the building process, God did some wonderful things; however, the enemy seemed to always find a way to stick his head up when we least expected it. A word of warning here.

> **When God is doing great things in the ministry, be assured that the enemy will take notice of it and do everything he can to hinder, and yes, even stop what the Lord is doing.**

One would think that the fight would come from those outside the church, but the sad fact is, many times it comes from within the church. I believe the psalmist David said it like this, *"For it was not an enemy that reproached me; then I could have borne it: neither was it he that hated me that did magnify himself against me; then I would have hid myself from him: But it was thou, a man mine equal, my guide, and mine acquaintance. We took sweet counsel together, and walked unto the house of God in company"* (Psalm 55:12-14 KJV). Such was our case.

It all started within our music ministry. Isn't it funny how the enemy always comes in through the music? Our attack came through a woman who attended another church in the community and was looking for a change. Maybe because of the exciting things she was hearing about the church throughout the community. Maybe it was because she was ready for something new and different. What I know and am convinced of now is that it was not the leading of the Lord as she so nicely proclaimed it to be. It is interesting how people invoke God into things and situations when it is convenient for them. We quickly found out that God had nothing to do with her leaving her church and coming to ours. I will admit it was exciting at first. You see the church was on the move. We were experiencing God's favor and blessings on every hand. Every area in the ministry was experiencing increase and abundance. We were breaking barriers in our youth and children's ministries and in the women and men's ministry. Our worship attendance and membership were up and the only area that could stand a little more attention was our music ministry. So, like many pastors who desire a good music program, we look for people who can help move us forward to that desire.

I interviewed her and everything on the surface looked and sounded good. I mean she was the leader of the community choir, a leader in the music ministry in her local church, and worked with the music department in the local school. She had an outstanding resume and could talk a good talk. All that was left was for me to contact her pastor and ask for her to be released from his church so that she and her family could join ours and become the leader of our music ministry. I sent the letter, and it wasn't long before we received a letter from her pastor who spoke highly of her abilities and work in the church. It was a letter that any pastor who had a good productive ministry team worker would have hated to write. It was a good letter and maybe that was the problem. It was too good, and I had no idea what we were getting.

We brought her in to work in the ministry with the music department, and things seemed to go well. However, we later discovered that she had personal issues that were affecting her leadership role and faithfulness to the church. I brought her in to discuss her situation with the hope of a good outcome, but to no avail. **Things got worse instead of better.** Now one of my requirements as the pastor was faithfulness, especially from the leadership team. If a person is not faithful, they should not be in a leadership role, and they should not be there for long. She started out being faithful, but over time, her faithfulness began to dwindle. I tried talking with her again, like any pastor who is concerned about his people, especially those whom they are leading. I said to her, if you don't think you can be faithful to the church, then you cannot serve in leadership over the music ministry. She got offensive, so much to the point that she began to stir up trouble within the church. She wrote letters to every church leader and put them in their mailboxes. The letters simply said something to the effect that the members of the church didn't know me, but they knew her. She had lived there all her life, and that her Holy Ghost didn't lead her wrong. She told them the money we had raised to buy property and build a church would be stolen by me while they slept, and that I and my family would pack up and leave town. When I got the news about what she had done, what she had said about me and my family, you can imagine how I felt as a new church pastor who moved his wife and little boys to a new city to do work for the Lord. **I was mad!** Yes, the preacher was mad. Don't judge me, because there may be things that you've been mad over before, and if you haven't, just keep living.

I told the church in that meeting, first of all, we were honest people; we would not take the church's money and leave town. We laid our lives on the line to come here to do what God had called us to do. I told them they should trust us, and if they didn't trust us, let us know, and the same truck, or one like it, that we used to come here, my wife and I would pack up our family and go back to our home in Fayetteville, 2 1/2 hours away.

The next course of action that I did was to have a meeting with the lady who started all the problems in the church. Of course, she decided that she wasn't going to come to a meeting that was set between me as the pastor, my church, and the pastor's council; therefore, she removed her membership from our church.

I want to say to you, just because you believe God has given you a vision and that vision is doing some great things in your life and the church, that doesn't mean that you will not experience problems. If it is the vision and purpose that God has put in your life, don't let the enemy cause you to abandon it. God will get the glory out of your faithfulness. You have to know without a shadow of a doubt, that God has called, anointed, and appointed you to serve the people you have; they will be blessed, and He will be glorified.

What was supposed to take five years happened in two. In 2005, we were entering into our new sanctuary to worship.

In our former church, the building seated about 130 people. This new facility has more than 500 seats, classroom spaces, office space, and a fellowship hall. It was just a phenomenal thing to see what God had done with our vision, and that the people had grabbed hold of it, and ran with it. But, like all things, you can't get complacent; you must still move forward. Training still had to be done. With this new facility, we had a responsibility to our new members.

We're in the new season of our lives. We're in a new church, and people are excited. God is blessing; people are being saved; the church is growing; and everything is wonderful. Know that if God gave you a vision to start, you still have to seek His face to continue what He started. Only He knows our beginning from the end. He already knows what it will look like when it's completed. However, we are still responsible for being steadfast in working, training, and developing to advance the kingdom of God.

The next phase was to recast the vision. This is the stage at which I believe many churches and leaders struggle. Just because God gave them a vision when the work first began, doesn't mean that vision will last forever without some attention.

God is in the business of acting, redeveloping, and reinstituting vision. What took place in the small sanctuary must continue in the larger space. Having more seats was wonderful, but now we are faced with the challenge of growing to fill them. So, how do you transition from 135 seats to more than 500? The people were excited to be in a new place of worship that offered more space for training and equipping for relevant ministry. One of our major emphases was on loving and serving people. We also focused our attention on loving and serving God. We changed our mission statement to one that reflected what we did as a church.

The mission of the church was changed for the last time. It reflects the Great Commission's mission to go into all the world and be disciples of Jesus Christ. We valued guest relations and made sure that every newcomer felt welcomed. When a person attended the church for the first time, they were considered our guests. The more they attended the more they were regarded as regular attenders. Our main focus was on family ministries, leadership development, and working with youth and children's ministries. Sunday morning children's church was done with intention, making sure that the worship was on their level and exciting. Our main worship experience was held in the sanctuary, and it too was impactful and engaging, with every message preached directed toward leading people to make a change in their lives to serve Jesus Christ.

However, before we could make any further progress, we had to be responsible and accountable for the level we were on at that time. We addressed needed changes and navigated seasons in ways that would positively impact people who wanted to connect with the church. Our leaders were trained and equipped to serve people and to work in the ministry before the Lord started sending people to us. We focused our attention on advancing the kingdom of God and the mission of the church, which spread throughout the community. It wasn't long until there was a noticeable change in the church and the community. Our impact as a church became widespread, so much so that the name Cornerstone was as common as a name of a major household appliance.

But like everything else, over a period of time, things begin to change, but not for the good. You see, we got comfortable and at ease. Before I knew it, the church was in stagnation mode. No souls were being saved, no new people were coming to join the church. There was no rotation in leadership. Members were not excited or enthusiastic about new programs. We were in trouble, and at first, I didn't even realize it. When I did begin to see the state of the church, I became frustrated. We were in a season of stagnation, and if something didn't happen soon, decline was sure to happen.

CHAPTER 4
THE NEED
FOR CHANGE

It was on a Monday evening in 2018 while I was serving on the Pathway Publications Board, I arrived in Cleveland, TN, for a board meeting, and checked into my hotel room at the Holiday Inn. When I got settled, I sat down and began to think about the church back home. It wasn't long before the enemy began to start showing me everything that was wrong with me and in the ministry. I started thinking about how this program didn't go as planned, how some people were not faithful. How ministry departments were unproductive, how some people sat and just looked lifeless at me while I preached. How, no new guests had attended the church in a while. How no one was getting saved, and how it seemed, the altar service was filled with the same people every Sunday.

It was like no one heeded the sermons of salvation, deliverance, and blessings I was preaching. All we were doing was helping them manage sin Sunday after Sunday. The church was in the stagnant stage of life, seemingly with no growth and no productivity. Maybe you have never been there as a pastor, but I am telling you, if not, just hold on because just as sure as there are good seasons of blessings and favor, **there will be seasons of change,** when it will seem like you can't nurture anything, or bring anything to life. When that feeling happens, you will be frustrated just like I was.

I knew I was called; I knew I was appointed; I had the appointment card in my wallet from the State Bishop. I knew I was anointed, but at that season in my life and ministry all I could think about was all the negative junk that the enemy was feeding me. I knew that I was the church's pastor, and I knew that I still had purpose in me. I'd go to the pulpit Sunday after Sunday and preach my heart out like nothing was wrong. I never told my wife. I didn't call my pastor friends and talk to them about the church. I didn't call the State Bishop and ask him to be reassigned to another church. Frustrated and hurt, I was leading while bleeding and doing it quite well because no one knew it.

I don't know who I'm talking to but maybe you are in a season of change in your life and ministry right now and you are feeling that same way. If you are, then let me encourage you to know that it's only a season. It does not matter how small or large your church is, the devil doesn't like it and he wants you to fail. I knew that God was not through with me, and He is not through with you either. I truly believe at that time, it was the enemy that was trying to get me to throw in the towel, but it was the Spirit of God on the inside of me that wouldn't let me quit.

The Lord reminded me of a message series I preached years ago found in 1 Kings, chapters 18 and 19. There, we find conflicting stories about a man of God— the Prophet Elijah. His first encounter was with King Ahab on Mt. Carmel where he called fire down from heaven and killed the prophets of Baal. I mean this man of God prayed a 58-word prayer and the fire of God fell from heaven and consumed the sacrifice, burned up the wood, stones, and dust, and even licked up the water. He then proceeded to kill all the false prophets of Baal. On that day, Elijah must have felt like a mighty man of valor. He experienced a season of change and victory. I mean the man was on cloud nine. I'm sure you can identify with him on days of great victory in your life and ministry.

But look what happened in the first three verses of the next chapter. Ahab goes home and tells his wicket wife Jezebel what the man of God did.

Ahab told Jezebel all that Elijah had done, also how he had executed all the prophets with the sword. Then Jezebel sent a messenger to Elijah saying, "So let the gods do to me and more also, if I do not make your life as the life of one of them by tomorrow about this time. And when he saw that, he arose and ran for his life (1 Kings 19:1-3 NKJV).

Elijah received a twenty-four-hour death threat on his life. Talk about seasons of change, this change didn't take three or four months; it was quick, fast, and in a hurry. Elijah heard that Jezebel (controlling spirit) threatened to do to him what he did to the prophets of Baal, and he was frightened.

The next thing you hear about this holy, anointed man of God is that he was on the run for his life. Not only was he on the run, but he prayed another prayer. The next prayer was quite different from the fire-falling, sacrifice-consuming, mountaintop prayer. He prayed that he might die. His response does not seem to be in alignment with the man of God who just prayed fire down from heaven and killed more than four hundred false prophets.

Why am I saying this? It's simple. There will be mountaintop experiences where we will experience victory, and then there will be days when we will be frustrated and want to run and hide. There will be moments when you taste sweet victory, and there will be moments when you will experience utter defeat.

Yes, even with all of God's anointed oil on us, with His divine presence and purpose in our lives, we will still have seasons of frustration. I call that "frustrated purpose!" Oh. I never told you the title of the message I preached. Here it is: "You didn't hire yourself; you can't fire yourself; and quitting is not an option."

God did three things for Elijah in 1 Kings, Chapter 19. Just as He did it for Elijah, and for me, I'm sure He will do it for you.

(1) He Refreshed Him: And as he lay and slept under a broom tree, suddenly an angel touched him and said to him, Arise and eat (v. 5 NKJV).

The Lord allowed Elijah to lie down and sleep. While he slept, God refreshed Him. No doubt while he slept God talked to him in dreams, letting him know that he was still His man. He probably told him everything would be alright.

(2) He Refueled Him: Then he looked, and there by his head was a cake baked on the coals, and a jar of water. So, he ate, drank, and layed down again. And the angel of the Lord came back the second time, and touched him, and said, *"Arise, eat, because the journey is too great for you"* (vv. 6-7 NKJV).

Here it is, the very first Angel Food cake. The Lord baked it for His servant while he slept. I don't know, but I'm inclined to believe that, that cake tasted like manna from heaven. Not only did he provide him with a cake, but He also provided him with life-sustaining water. This cake and water were God's way of telling him, that He was his sustainer. Just as the Lord did for Elijah, He will do the same for us when faced with demonic forces that want to stop what He is doing.

(3) He Refired Him: *And he arose, and ate and drank; and he went in the strength of that food forty days and forty nights as far as Horeb, the mountain of God* (v. 8 NKJV).

God gave Elijah what he needed to get to his next assignment. Just as He did it for him, He will do it for us. Frustrated purpose will happen to all of us at some point in our lives. Regardless of where we are, how large or small our church is, or how anointed we may think we are, there will be seasons of change, both good and not so good. What is most important, is that we are aware of how to navigate and keep moving forward for God and His purpose. Now back to my story.

So, I'm sitting there in my hotel room with a mind of "stinking thinking" about me and my church, and I began to talk to the Lord. I knew He would hear me; I mean He always does. However, this time was different. His response was not what I expected. I'm looking for a little sympathy and maybe a little compassion. After all, He is a compassionate God. Oh, but not this time.

This time He told me: "It's your fault." I wasn't expecting to hear that, at least not from God. Now, I was surprised to hear that it was my fault. I didn't want to hear that. But He said to me again, "It's your fault!" So, I said to Him, What do you mean, it's my fault? He replied: "What's happening at your church is all on you." (He said this to me.) "You can sit, sulk, and sour here all you want to, but until you change your attitude about your church, nothing else will change." He said, "I have given you everything you need to move your church forward."

For the rest of that evening, it was me and Him in that room. It reminded me of my first encounter with Him when I was assigned to pastor the church in February 2002.

What I am about to share with you will literally transform your life and ministry, I know it did mine. It all started with a series of questions that He asked me. As you read them, ask yourself the same questions He asked me. You may want to grab a pen and paper because what you read, you will want to write down, as it will reveal some things about you.

The first thing the Lord said to me was, "Do you remember how you started when you first received the position as the pastor of the church in 2002? How I gave you a vision; how you put together a plan of action; then you went before the church and cast that vision to the church—first to the leaders, and then to the congregation? The vision and plan were to train and equip leaders/laity, build strong families, and impact your community. Your focus was all about equipping the members to do the work of the ministry. Not only were you the pastor, but you were also their example of a servant leader. The church embraced the vision and plan, and growth was spontaneous, so much so that the projected time of building a new worship facility was shortened by three years. The Lord said to me, you projected that after working the vision, the church would need to purchase land and build a new worship center. The vision and plan you put forth was big and aggressive, but the people had a mind to work, and they did. You told the people that it would take five years before the church would need to build new facilities. However, what was supposed to take five years happened in two. That was because of vision, planning and equipping the members.

After moving to the new facility, you continued to cast vision, train, and equip the members, and the church experienced growth. However, as you got comfortable,

> "Change is the law of life. And those who look only to the past or present are certain to miss the future."
> ------- John F. Kennedy

you forgot the things that produced growth and success. The excitement of ministry became routine and all about doing church. Ministry still took place, but the need to continue vision casting and training was no longer a priority. The Lord said, you got busy doing church instead of building people. The church was experiencing a season of change and you had not equipped the members to handle it. We had become experts at doing church and forgot what it meant to do ministry.

CHAPTER 5
FRUSTRATED
PURPOSE

The Bible gives several examples of leaders who suffered with frustrated purpose. Let's look at a couple. One in the Old Testament and the other in the New Testament.

The first leader we will look at is *Moses the deliverer.* When we look at this man of God and how God used him to deliver His people out of bondage, we see that he suffered with what I call *frustrated purpose.* Moses was called, appointed, and anointed by God with purpose. That purpose was larger than any mere man could ever do without the help of God. All one would have to do is just examine the course of this man's journey from the time of his birth until the time of his death.

Chapter two of the Book of Exodus describes the birth and early life of Moses. His mother, a Hebrew slave named Jochebed, defied the order of Pharaoh that all Hebrew Jewish males die at birth. She hid her son for three months until she could hide him no longer. Once he was too old to hide any longer, she placed him in a basket among the reeds of the Nile River, under the watchful eye of his sister. It was there that Pharaoh's daughter found and took him home with her. She hired the Hebrew slave to be his wet nurse who happened to be his birth mother to take care of him. Once weaned, he was returned to be raised in the palace as an Egyptian prince with the best education as a son of Egypt.

At the age of forty, he found out that he was of the Hebrew Jewish lineage by birth. One day he returned to his birthplace to his people where he encountered an Egyptian soldier badly mistreating a Hebrew slave. In a heated altercation, he killed the soldier and fled from Egypt to the desert where he married the daughter of Jethro, the priest of Midian. For the next forty years, he was on the backside of the desert, tending to his father-in-law's sheep. One day he came to Horeb, the mountain of God, and saw smoke rising from a bush that was on fire but not consumed. Out of the bush, the voice of God spoke to him to remove his shoes because the ground he was standing on was holy ground. It was there that he had his encounter with God and received his assignment to return to Egypt to free the Hebrew people who were under the bondage of Pharaoh and the Egyptians.

Through a series of meetings and plagues before the Pharaoh, God used Moses to free His people. Moses whose name means "deliverer" became God's man of purpose. His responsibility was to get a nation of people from a place and lifestyle of bondage to a land and lifestyle of plenty, more than enough. The Bible describes it as Canaan, the land that flowed with milk and honey. You would have thought this would be an easy chore. The Hebrew people saw the miracles of God; they saw the ten plagues that led up to their Exodus from Egypt, and they were on their way as a nation to a land promised by God. They were guided by a cloud by day and a pillar of fire by night—Moses' first real test as the new leader of more than 600,000 men, not counting women and children. The population could have been four times that size, or 2.4 million. Can you imagine pastoring a church this size?

Moses is now the new leader of this nation of people. His first encounter with frustrated purpose as a leader happened at the Red Sea. Well let's say just for the sake of leading people, Moses was their pastor. He was called and appointed by God, which meant he was purposed by God. Undoubtedly, God knew he had what it took to fulfill the assignment given to him. However, this would not come without challenges and frustrations. At the Red Sea, Pastor Moses would experience his frustration. I believe this was just the beginning of the many times he would get frustrated.

The first account of the people complaining was at the Red Sea, *"Leave us alone that we may serve the Egyptians. For it would have been better for us to serve the Egyptians than to die in the wilderness"* (Exodus 14:9-31 NASB)

They saw the Red Sea roll back on two sides and they walked across dry land. After the last person stepped out of the seabed on the other side, they saw the waters roll back, closing the path in the sea. They saw Pharaoh, his army, horses, and charioteers drown. We read in Exodus 15 how Miriam the prophetess, Aaron's sister, took a tambourine, and all the other women followed her with tambourines, dancing and singing to

God! What a victory! He pitched "horse and rider into the sea." What was supposed to be about an eleven-day trip to the Land of Promise turned into a forty-year voyage with only their children entering.

Up until now, Moses understood his assignment, and I believe he was fully committed to the task. However, three days later, he would experience his next challenge of dealing with people who soon forgot all that God had done for them and just how good God was. They arrived at a place called Marah. Marah got its name because all the water there was bitter. I can imagine more than 600,000 men, women, and children plus livestock walking for three days and finding neither a place to rest nor receive refreshing water. They couldn't drink the water. So, what do the people do? Well, they did what some people do when things don't go the way that they think they should have gone. They complained. Yes, even in the church. Remember now, I pastored for more than twenty years, and I'm a witness. Please understand, I'm not saying everyone, but there are always one or two and sometimes that's all that's needed to get everyone else on board.

After seeing all that God had done and all that Pastor Moses had done, the very next thing you see in the text is, "Then the people complained and turned against Moses." So, what does any good pastor do? Well, we do the same thing Moses did. Moses cried to the Lord for help, and the Lord responded to Moses' cry. The Lord showed him a tree which he threw into the water, and it was made sweet.

I wish I could tell you that was the end of the people complaining to Moses. No, this was just the beginning of a long list of people complaining to him. Let's explore several others.

The people complained about being hungry; God provided manna and quail meat (Exodus 16:1-7, 11-12). The people complained about being thirsty, God provided water (Exodus 17:1-7). The people complained about Moses' absence and forsook the Lord by creating a golden calf and altar (Exodus 32:1-8). The Lord ordered the Levites to kill 3,000 people by the sword, because they worshiped the golden calf (Exodus 32:1-28). The people complained about adversity and food (Numbers 11). Moses was displeased and wanted to die (vv. 10-15). The Lord sent a very great plague (v. 33).

Pastor Moses was so frustrated that He wanted to die. To make matters even worse, not only were the people complaining and murmuring, but now Moses's brother and sister have joined the dissidents. Miriam and Aaron complained about Moses' leadership. The Lord cursed Miriam with leprosy for seven days (Numbers 12:1-15). The people complained about how difficult it looked to enter the Promised Land, so they refused to enter (Numbers 14:1-9). The people complained again and wanted to kill Moses and tried to select another leader (Numbers 14:10-38). Several years later, key leaders rebelled against Moses. God opened the earth, and it swallowed them up, *"All the men who belonged to Korah"* (v. 32)! The people complained again and they accused Moses of killing God's people. God killed

14,700 people (Numbers 16:41-50).

Pastor Moses' frustration got the best of him 19 years later. The people contented with him again because of no water. Moses struck the rock instead of speaking to it as instructed by the Lord. God provided the water; however, this act of disobedience would cost him dearly. *He would not be allowed to complete his assignment of bringing the people to the Promised Land, but only seeing it* (Numbers 20: 1-12). "But the Lord said to Moses and Aaron, *"Because you have not believed Me, to treat Me as holy in the sight of the sons of Israel, therefore you shall not bring this assembly into the land which I have given them"* (v.12 NASB1995).

Let me stop here and encourage every pastor who knows without doubt that God has called, anointed, and appointed you to lead people to the Promised Land—Heaven—to remain faithful to your assignment. Even when people become unreasonable, unrealistic, and unrelentless to the point of complaining and grumbling. Do your best not to allow it to cause you to disobey God, thereby forfeiting your inheritance of God's promise. I've been there, and I know it's not easy leading people who try to find any reason to complain even when you have their best interest at heart. I'll be the first to say it is frustrating to say the least. But, keep your Godly composure, you have been called and purposed to do what you are doing.

The final act of the people complaining against God and Moses (Numbers 21:4-9). God sent fiery serpents and "many people of Israel died" (v. 6). What a tragedy, what a shame!

Now, let's look at another person who was called, anointed, and appointed to lead people. He was also frustrated, but he didn't allow his frustration to get the best of him. He remained faithful to his assignment.

"Let him that would move the world first move himself." — Socrates

I believe Socrates was on to something when he made that statement. While it is true without doubt that we live in an ever-increasing world of change, it is also true that if you hope to make the best out of moments of change, it must first start with you. (Man, did I ever have to learn that.) God really does use people to facilitate change, and it all starts within you. More specifically, in your mind.

Progress is impossible without change, and those who cannot change their minds cannot change anything.

That part of you where the Enemy wants to dictate and control you—the mind—is the real place where spiritual warfare takes place: battles of self-esteem—how you feel about yourself—self-concept—what you think about yourself—and self-worth—how you value yourself. It is of the utmost importance that you have a healthy feeling about who you are, how you think about yourself, and just as equally important is how you value yourself. To think well about who you are will make a world of difference in your physical and emotional health. One of the reasons people suffer with health issues has a lot to do with how they feel, think, and value themselves. It is just as important that you do not put too much stock in how other people feel, think, and value you as well. To do that, could quite possibly give others too much power over you. When that happens, you will find yourself pleasing others sometimes to your own detriment. Please understand, I'm not saying that you shouldn't value how others feel, think, or value you. I'm just saying you should value yourself more.

Therefore, any changes you make should be brought about because you desire to live, be healthy, thrive, and be happy. Inspire to be all that God has purposed and designed you to be. This kind of change will not happen overnight, and many times is not instantaneous. It will take time, consistency, and determination on your part.

> Even if you cannot change all the people around you, you can change the people you choose to be around. Life is too short to waste your time on people who don't respect, appreciate, and value you. Spend your life with people who make you smile, laugh, and feel loved." Surround yourself among people who are inspirational.
> — Roy T. Bennett,
> The Light in the Heart

The slogan for The National Negro Association for the Advancement of Colored People (NAACP) is "A mind is a terrible thing to waste." That statement is true as it relates to education; however, it is also true in every part of one's life. What is even more important, it relates to the life of every believer. You see, it was God who created the mind in the beginning. He created it with the express purpose that man would use it to serve Him. The reality is that man has become wise in his own mind and therefore many times serving God is not the priority. The Word of God tells us: *"If any man be in Christ, he is a new creature: old things are passed away; behold, all things are become new"* (2 Corinthians 5:17 KJV). That starts with a mind to make the change from an old life to a new one. It is that change that puts man back in right standing with the loving Father God who has plans for us. Change must start with the individual. Take a peek inside your mind. It has been said that,

"True change takes place in the imagination."
— Unknown

However, we must be careful not to allow our imagination to run wild. We are told to gird up the loins of our mind, be sober, perfectly hope for the grace being brought to you at the revelation of Jesus Christ (see 1 Peter 1:13).

Mind is defined as: The intellectual or intelligent power in man; the understanding; the power that conceives, judges, or reasons.

Another meaning is, "Intention; purpose; design. Inclination; will; desire" (n.)

"To attend to; to fix the thoughts on; to regard with attention." (v.t.)

Change is an inside job! If it never happens within, it will never manifest without. Watch your thoughts, they will dictate your actions; watch your actions, they will form your behaviors; watch your behaviors, they will dictate your destiny.

> **"If we don't change, we don't grow. If we don't grow, we aren't really living."**
> **—Gail Sheehy**

God wants us to change our minds. What we think, consciously and subconsciously, continually dictates how we feel: love, peace, joy, hope, and a sense of purpose, on the one hand, or fear, anxiety, anger, isolation, depression, and aimlessness on the other hand.

Do not conform to the pattern of this world but be transformed by the renewing of your mind. Then you will be able to test and approve what God's will is—his good, pleasing, and perfect will" (see Romans 12:2).

That is why God works on the mind of man. The agent of change for the believer is the Holy Spirit. He makes all things new.

> **"The measure of intelligence is the ability to change"**
> **—Albert Einstein**

"You were taught, with regard to your former way of life, to put off your old self, which is being corrupted by its deceitful desires; to be made new in the attitude of your

minds; and to put on the new self, created to be like God in true righteousness and holiness" (Ephesians 4:22-24 NIV).

CHAPTER 6
CHANGE
STARTS WITH YOU

Lost Your Way?

Let me ask a few questions. Have you lost your way? Has the church you pastor or the ministry you lead lost its way? Has it become consumed with doing church instead of experiencing ministry? If so, could it be that you have lost your way? It's easy to do, especially if you are a long-term pastor at your current church. Please don't misunderstand what I'm saying. I do believe that there are many benefits of being a long-term pastor. However, there are some disadvantages as well. Just wanted to point out that serving as a long-term pastor in the same church could have the likelihood of becoming complacent and caught in stagnation, especially, if a new vision is not being cast on a regular basis. Believe me when I say, the longer you serve in one church, the easier it becomes routine with little freshness and newness. When that happens, frustration and burnout happens. I am a prime example, serving as the lead pastor over one church for more than twenty years. I will talk more about this in a later chapter.

For now, let me tell you how the Lord helped me. It all started with a series of questions. These really hit home for me. Here they are...

Question One: Who Are You?

So, here's where God got my attention in that hotel room on the 4th floor of the Holiday Inn in Cleveland, TN. He asked me four questions. *The first question was, "Who are you?"* Now before you answer that question, think about it for a few moments. My answer to that was just like many who are posed the same question. I began to tell God that I'm a preacher, pastor, husband, father, brother, friend, district overseer, and the list went on. I'm telling God all this, and He asks me again, "Who are you?"

He said to me, you are telling me all the things that you do. He said, "What you do is not who you are." You do what you do because of who you are, but they don't define you. The moment you allow what you do to define you, that will be the time when you lose who you are. When that happens, and you are no longer able to do those things, or if a season of change stops you, you will become frustrated and then, maybe even lost.

You see, like many others, I had gotten wrapped up in all the things that I did, and lost to who I was. I quickly began to realize that before I was ever a preacher, pastor, husband, father, brother, friend, district overseer, I was James Scott McIntyre, and I'm created in God's image and likeness. Therefore, He defines me, not what I did. I am fearfully and wonderfully made. I am unique, one of a kind as no one else has my DNA. I'm my mom's oldest child, a black American male, the oldest of four siblings. I'm an extrovert. I'm funny, smart, and a person of character and integrity. I am people-oriented, which means I like being around people. I am passionate about family. I like fishing, sports, especially playing golf, soul-food, having fun, reading, Westerns and old movies. This is who I was before I ever started doing the things that I do. The truth is that many of the things that make me who I am, I really enjoy. However, there have been times that I got so caught up in what I do, that I lost myself. Please don't misunderstand what I am saying. Whatever I do, I give it my all; and sometimes, I feel guilty for taking time for myself to do the things I enjoy. I have learned now to take some time and just relax, go play a round of golf, or just do nothing, if that's what I decide.

Let me encourage you, if you lost who you are, rediscover yourself. You will find that life and ministry can be so fulfilling. Then He asked me question number two.

Question Two: What Do You Do?

The next question the Lord asked me was easy. You see, I was at that time, as well as now, more acquainted with what I do as opposed to who I am. At least I should have been, especially since I was the one doing it. I'm sure you can define what you do better than anyone else. Especially, since you are the one doing it, and it's our default question when we are asked, who we are.

First of all, and without question, I am a husband, father and grandfather. These three positions are primarily important and first place in my life. You see, there was a time that was not the case. I allowed other things and people to have that space, and it caused some real problems for me and my family. Yes, even the church. I will speak more about that later. Over the past several years, what I do has changed as it relates to the positions, jobs, and responsibilities that I held and some I hold now.

At the time the Lord asked me these questions, I was serving as the Executive Pastor at Cornerstone Family Worship Center Church of God and President/Chief Executive Officer of Cornerstone Community-Based Programs in Washington, North Carolina, where my wife, Lisa, and I served for twenty-one years. I also served as the Pamlico District Overseer, on the Eastern North Carolina State Council (ENC), ENC Ministerial Internship Board, Church Plant Revitalization Board, ENC Home for Children's Board of Trustees, and Pathway Press Board of Trustees. In addition to these ministry assignments, I also served on several community boards and committees in the county where we lived. Just to name a few: The Beaufort County Chamber of Commerce, Partnership for Children Executive Board, BC360 Leadership Board, Advisory to Superintendent of Schools, and Interfaith Community Board.

As I was contemplating my next steps, I began to pour my heart out to God and ask for guidance. I reflected on my past experiences where I held various leadership positions such as a pastor, district overseer, and executive director for a community-based program.

Prior to my transition to the International Headquarters, I served on thirteen different boards and committees at one time. I had no idea. However, God's response to me was to not get lost in what I do because of who I am. It made me realize that I had been so caught up in my work that I had forgotten my true purpose, which is to glorify God. Every pastor and leader should ask themselves this question: "What do I do?" My main goal is to bring glory to God with everything I do. I don't mind telling you, there were days when I failed miserably, but I never quit.

One of those times was in 2009 on a Wednesday night at a church meeting. That year was a difficult season for our church. We experienced many challenges and a real season of change for me personally and for the church. During that meeting, things got very heated between me and another member of the church. As a matter of fact, things got so bad that the situation almost developed into a fistfight between me and the member. I can honestly say that if my wife, Lisa, had not been there sitting right in the pew in front of the man, things might have ended a different way. The crazy thing about it was, I had just completed a month series of preaching and teaching on "Be angry and sin not," found in Ephesians 4:26. *"Be ye angry, and sin not: let not the sun go down upon your wrath: Neither give place to the devil"* (KJV). That one night's events set our church back two years. That season was the most challenging of all my twenty-one years of pastoring. That night I almost lost it all in just a matter of minutes.

I am sure you can imagine the talk and rumors that went around our community. Despite my best efforts, the church experienced a season of negative change in the community. As the pastor, it was a tough pill to swallow, but I knew that we had the power to make a change. I don't mind telling you how difficult it was for me to go to the pulpit every Sunday morning, but change must start with me. Once I shifted my mind and embraced the idea that I did not have to do it, but instead I had the privilege of doing things, it made all the difference. As a leader, it's important to remember that blessings and favor from God don't come from focusing solely on the work we do, but from the changes we make and the positive impact we have in the lives of others for the glory of God. Which brings me to the next question the Lord asked me.

Question Three: Why Do You Do It?

Without a doubt, I believe this is the most important of all the questions He asked me. There could conceivably be many reasons why we do what we do. However, if they don't all lead back to the main reason, we could find ourselves spinning our wheels. At the very least, not living up to our true purpose and potential. The thing about purpose is that it is dictated by the person who created and assigned it. Purpose is defined as, "Why you do something or why something exists."

So, here's what I said to God. "My true purpose and ultimate reason for doing what I do is out of love and obedience and to bring You glory." Matthew said: *"Let your light so shine before men, that they may see your good works, and glorify your Father which is in heaven"* (5:16). To that He replied, What does that look like? Here is what I said as a pastor, preaching and teaching the good news of the gospel to a lost world. It is . . .

- Discipling new converts to know how to live a victorious life pleasing to the Lord.
- Teaching them what it means to have a relationship with the Lord and the body of Christ.
- Teaching them how to be good stewards in terms of their gifting and talents for the Lord and church.

In short, it is called what I refer to as the Ephesian model.

And truly He gave some to be apostles, and some to be prophets, and some to be evangelists, and some to be pastors and teachers, for the perfecting of the saints, for the work of the ministry, for the edifying of the body of Christ. And this until we all come into the unity of the faith and of the knowledge of the Son of God, to a full-grown man, to the measure of the stature of the fullness of Christ (Ephesians 4:11-13).

It is important that we understand the real purpose of why we do what we do. The moment we lose our purpose, we lose everything. Purpose is what grounds us when seasons of frustration, burnout, discouragement, and despair set in. Purpose is what gives us energy to keep going when everything else around us says give up and throw in the towel. Purpose is what drives us to go further and do more for God. When life challenges and ministry difficulties become overwhelming, purpose is what gives us the strength to keep worshiping and serving God. Without purpose, ministry would become mundane and meaningless.

Purpose is what compelled Jesus to fulfill his divine assignment and to finish what the Father God had given Him to do. *"Jesus said to them, My food is to do the will of Him who sent Me, and to finish His work"* (John 4:34 NKJV). Ultimately that is the responsibility of every servant leader.

Let me ask you, why do you do what you do? What is your purpose? Is it what the Creator designed for you to do? Does it bring glory to God? Does it equip the saints to do the work of ministry? The final question proposed to me by God was one that is soul-searching. It ultimately spoke to the conclusion at the end of this life.

Question Four: What Do You Hope to Gain by Doing What You Do?

This question can be answered in several ways. As a pastor, my first thought had nothing to do with me but for the people I served. To consider any benefits for me before those in my care would seem selfish. My desire is to see those whom I have had the privilege to serve grow into committed, mature, and victorious disciples of Christ. My hope is that I've done my duties as a pastor so well that my followers will equip those who come along behind them to be disciples of Jesus Christ as well. *"And the things that thou hast heard of me among many witnesses, the same commit thou to faithful men, who shall be able to teach others also"* (2 Timothy 2:2 KJV).

Then I turned my attention to what I pray and desire to hear Him say when my work here is done. It is what every believer desires to hear Him say. The apostle Paul sums it up at the end of his journey.

"For I am already being poured out, and the time of my release is here. I have fought the good fight, I have finished the course, I have kept the faith. Now there is laid up for me the crown of righteousness, which the Lord, the righteous Judge, shall give me at that Day; and not to me only, but also to all those who love His appearing" (see 2 Timothy 4:6-8).

"Well done, good and faithful servant, enter into the joy of the Lord" (see Matthew 25:21).

After a stern rebuking and answering the questions of who I am, what I do, why I do it, and what do I hope to gain from doing it, the Lord then said to me; now that you have found your way, when you return home, ask your church these same questions and lead them back to finding their way.

The Lord said to me, "Stop focusing on your season of frustration, and look at the purpose and potential I have given you." The culture of the ministry is set by you. He then provided me with a new fresh vision to take back to the church—one that was fresh, inspiring, and exciting. It was one that would lead our church into a new relaunch for future growth and productivity. That vision breathed life back into me. It was a vision that would work in any size church. In the next few chapters, I will unfold the vision and plan that was revealed to me and how it transformed our church. But before I do, let's take a little time and talk about vision.

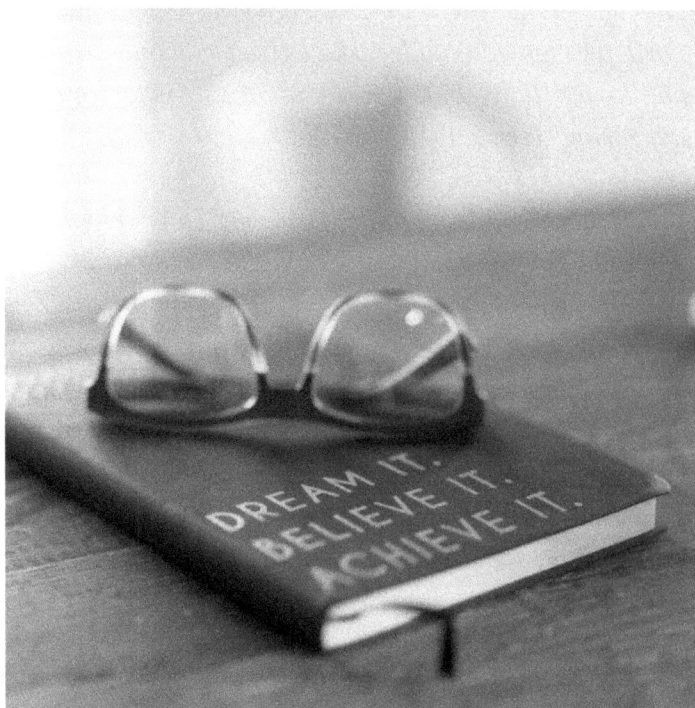

CHAPTER 7
VISION FOR
CHANGE

In this ever-changing world, churches who are experiencing stagnation, decline, and headed to extinction-there is good news for you. I started early in my ministry recognizing that if I was going to be successful, the way God designed for me to be successful, then I had to depend totally upon Him. I had to be led by Him and by His Spirit. I had to listen closely to His voice and push out all the others. You see, there will be a lot of voices that will speak into your ear, and if you're not focused on His voice, then you will not do what He called you to do. So, I learned that if I'm going to be able to do what God has put in my heart, then I must rely on Him. The same is true if you are going to experience change in whatever ministry assignment He calls you to do. You must recognize and depend on God. He has the master plan for what He called you to do. It's His vision, we are just His laborers.

Webster defines *vision* as, "the faculty or state of being able to see. The ability to think about or plan the future with imagination or wisdom." Oh, but vision is more than that. You see, I believe that vision comes from God. It is His divine plan for you, your family, and your ministry. *"For I know the thoughts that I think toward you, saith the LORD, thoughts of peace, and not of evil, to give you an expected end"* (Jeremiah 29:11 KJ21).

"Where there is no vision, the people perish: but he that keepeth the law, happy is he" (Proverbs 29:18 KJ21).

We are instructed in Scripture to: *"Write the vision, and make it plain upon tablets, that he may run that readeth it. For the vision is yet for an appointed time, but at the end it shall speak, and not lie. Though it tarry, wait for it; because it will surely come, it will not tarry".* (Habakkuk 2:2-3 KJ21).

The prophet Habakkuk tells us to write the vision and make it plain, that those who see it may run with it. But before he says that he first says in verse one; *"I will stand upon my watch, and set me upon the tower, and will watch to see what he will say unto me, and what I shall answer when I am reproved"*(Habakkuk 2:1 KJ21). This verse is the key to doing whatever God has asked you to do. You must stand your watch, in other words, be in place and I might add, ***the right place.*** Afterwards, you must be open and free from distractions to hear what the Lord will say. Every word of it. For it is too important to slip up. I understood this from the very first day that I took the role of the pastor of the West 9th Street Church of God. It all started with a vision from God. See, I realized that if, again, I was going to be able to do what God had put in my heart for Him, and those He put into my care, it would be through Him that I would get my instructions. Here is how it all started.

It was in February of 2002 when I assumed the role as the lead pastor of the West 9th Street Church of God. Up until that day, I was employed by one of the largest office dealerships on the East Coast. I was also a member of The Abundant Life Church of God, under the leadership of my pastor and spiritual father, Bishop James C. Monroe, Jr. There we served in several ministry positions and on the leadership team. My wife, Lisa, and I along with our three sons, James, Jr., Jonathan, and Joshua, were living in a nice middle-class neighborhood in Fayetteville, NC. We were doing quite well for ourselves, enjoying life. Not only were we serving at the church, but we also served as leaders in our district, as well as on state-level programs. So, we were quite busy with work and in the ministry. Let me pause and say this. *God is not looking for lazy people, He is looking for those who are already active in doing something that is meaningful.* Okay, now back to my story.

One Sunday evening after getting home from an evening worship service, Lisa and I were preparing for bed when our home phone rang. The voice on the other end was our State Bishop Paul Clawson, at that time. I still remember his raspy voice saying to me after our greeting, Brother James McIntyre, you are now the new pastor of the West 9th Street Church of God.

To that, I replied, "Oh, my God!" Well, after a few more words, he prayed for me, then we hung up. I turned to my wife who asked me who was on the phone and said the same things he said to me. To that she replied, "Oh, my God!" Here we are the new pastors of our first church, and it is almost three hours away from where we lived and worked. I remember telling my boss at the company where I'd worked for twenty years that we had been appointed to a church in another city which was three hours away. His words to me were, "Can't they find a church closer to here?"

My wife, Lisa, experienced the same thing when she told her boss, which happened to be at our youngest son Joshua's primary school. I will tell you that we had no idea what to expect. All we knew was that God had opened a door, and we were going to walk through it, and we did.

Therefore, we started packing in preparation to move to another city away from family, friends, work, and our beloved church. Not knowing if the people in our new assignment would welcome or even receive us. It was difficult for all of us, especially our sons. To make the transition a little easier we waited until school was out for the summer break for our move. James, our oldest, had the most difficult time of the three with the move. You see he was in high school and had many friends and the thought of having to leave his friends in his last year of high school was hard for him. Still, we moved forward by the leading of God and His new plans for our lives. We began transitioning from Fayetteville, NC moving to Washington, NC, which was at that time a little more than a three-hour drive. Wow, moving more than two hundred miles away from the place of your birth, family, church, and friends, all that we knew and loved.

Prior to moving, I will never forget my first trip to Washington as the new pastor of the church. It was on Thursday morning. As I drove the three-hour trip there, I remember the last 18-mile stretch between Greenville, NC and Washington, NC seemed like the longest drive of my life. I remember after getting there, I checked into my room at the Comfort Inn, and because I was very tired from the trip, I laid down on the bed for what I thought would be a quick nap. I remember saying to God, Lord, you have me here for a reason, I don't quite know what it is, except for pastoring a church. Since that is the case, then you are going to have to help me. I asked Him to please give me a vision for this church. Not long after saying those words, I drifted off to sleep. While I slept, the Lord spoke to me in a dream, which was the first of several visions for the church. I remember waking up and going to the desk sitting across the room, and on that desk was a little pencil and a pad. I sat down and began to write what the Lord shared with me while I slept.

You see, what I dreamed of was His vision for the church. It consisted of first and foremost, simply loving His people, discipleship, children and youth ministry, leadership training, orderly worship experiences, and finally community engagement. Well, I wrote it all down and prepared for my first meeting as the new pastor of the West 9th Street Church of God.

Later that evening, I arrived at the church for the meeting, I was greeted by several members who welcomed me as the new pastor. One of those who received me was the head deacon of the church, William

Godley. This was not my first time meeting him. We met a few weeks prior on my first trip to the church to preach during the pastoral search process. On that occasion, I remember him saying to me these words, "I don't know if you are going to get this church, whether it's you or not, whoever it is, he said I'm going to work with them. To that I replied, "I don't know either, but thank you for telling me that." Well, I was the one who did receive the appointment as the new pastor.

Now back to my first meeting with the congregation. If you would have been there at that meeting, you probably would have said something like this, "This guy will not last here a month." First of all, I had been appointed to follow a long-term pastor, Bishop Julius N. Geiger, who had served the church for more than thirty years. Secondly, I was a brand-new pastor; this was my very first church. Oh, I had a few months of experience as an associate pastor, but not a lead pastor. Lastly, despite the advice given to new pastors not to change anything significantly for at least a year, I went ahead and made drastic changes in that very first meeting. Looking back, I realize it was a bold move, but I believed that God had assigned me to help the church move from a stagnant position and meet the needs of both the church and the community.

I shared my vision with the church, and from that process, I made many changes, including moving Sunday school from 10 a.m. back to 9:30 a.m. and worship service from 12 noon to 11:30 a.m. After a little tension, that went through all right. However, after the next change, you would have thought I was the enemy. It involved those who would be preaching on Sunday mornings. I mean it would make sense that the pastor should be the person who fills the pulpit on Sunday morning. I just thought that since I was the pastor, I would be the one doing the preaching. Well, when I said that, it was like the house went up in flames. Let me put this in context, so you can understand. I was told that evening that the church had many other ministers who also filled the pulpit on Sunday morning. These ministers preached on youth Sunday, on women's Sunday, and on brothers' Sunday. Which left only one or possibly two Sundays a month, depending on if the month had five weeks. So, I said again, I will be filling the pulpit every Sunday morning. Again, that didn't go over well at all.

Now here I am, in my first pastorate, in a new town having my first meeting with a congregation who has a membership of mostly senior adults who look to be older than I am. Not to mention that some of them had been in church longer than I had been in the world. This was a major change for the church. None of those in the meeting that evening objected to the change of service schedule or the way we would be collecting the offerings, which we made earlier that evening. So, what did I do? How did I handle it? Well, I did what any good Church of God pastor would do in a situation like this. I reverted to the Church of God Book of Minutes. I asked everyone who was a minister in the church to stand up, thirteen people both male and female stood. Then the Lord said to me, have everyone who does not have Church of God credentials have a seat. Only three people were left standing. I asked them to have a seat, and then I said these words to the entire church. The Church of God Book of Minutes says that if you do not have credentials, you are not supposed to stand behind the pulpit.

Now that really got things stirred up. So, I said to them, "I'm not going to treat you that way because I didn't call you, God did. However, as your pastor, it is my job to affirm that calling." Then I said this: "My litmus test is the same as God's and it's one word, it's called faithfulness. God requires faithfulness, so I will require it as well." I said to the ministers that, if you are faithful, you will have every opportunity to minister in this church, but if you are not faithful, you won't even have a chance to pray, read a scripture or minister in this church. What I did not say was preach. I made that very clear. I said, if you are faithful, you have every opportunity to serve, and I said faithfulness is the litmus test that I believe God gives every one of us.

Another major change was how the church received offerings. Now this may not mean much to you, but it was very important to me and the vision that the Lord had given me for the church. You see I learned a long time ago that with God's vision there will come His provision. For what the Lord had given me for the church would take His provision to see it accomplished. I was told that night that the church was taking up six offerings on Sunday morning. Let's see. There were the tithes, public offering, sick offering, dollar march, missions offering, and a speaker offering for the person who preached for the pastor. I jokingly say now, that was a change I probably should not have made. Well, we moved from the six offerings to what I called, giving on purpose. As the pastor, I believed that it was my responsibility to lead the church in giving. So, I said to the members that I would lead in giving and that I would never ask them to give something that I was not willing to give.

In addition to tithes and offerings, there were many special offerings, and because the members saw me give, they gave. Before we knew it, our income seemingly tripled in a matter of months. By the end of the year, we had raised and deposited over one hundred thousand dollars. We were well on our way to buying property and building our new church.

After several more suggested changes and some discussion, I was able to continue sharing the vision as the Lord had given me earlier that day. By the time the meeting ended, the members were calling me pastor. I spent the next several months working on the vision by training and equipping my leadership team and providing assistance to other leaders who needed it.

I remember telling the church that if we do all the Lord put in my heart to do, within five years we would have to buy land and build, because our current facility would not be able to hold the people He would send us.

What was supposed to take five years, happened in two short years.

I remember sitting in the pulpit on Sunday morning and looking over the congregation in the church that was filled without room. Seeing people through the window in the door that led to the foyer come in, look to see if there was a seat only to find none. They would turn around and head back out the front door. As a way to fix that problem, we started a children's church which was held in the church's fellowship hall, and a nursery was held in my assistant's office. It wasn't long before our children and youth ministry was averaging more than forty in attendance, and our church was filled with hungry worshipers every Sunday. Our mid-week service was filled as well. God was up to something, and the church was on the move. It all started with a vision from God, and people who believed in what some said was impossible.

Let's unpack this thing called **VISION:**

VISION: the faculty or state of being able to see. The ability to think about or plan the future with imagination or wisdom. Not only is it being able to think about a plan, but also being able to share and work the plan.

VISION: Hebrew: haza, to "perceive"; Greek: harao; to "see." Vision is a supernatural presentation of certain scenery or circumstances to the mind of a person while awake.

Vision experiences are similar to dreams through which supernatural insight or awareness is given by revelation from God. The difference between a dream and a vision is that dreams occur only during sleep, while visions can happen while a person is awake or asleep. The purpose of visions is to give guidance and direction to God's servants and to foretell the future.

In the Bible, people who had visions were filled with a special consciousness of God. The most noteworthy examples in the Old Testament of recipients of visions are Ezekiel and Daniel. Visions in the New Testament are most prominent in the Gospel of Luke, the Book of Acts, and the Book of Revelation.

The Word of God tells us: *"Where there is no vision, the people perish"* (Proverbs 29:18 KJ21). Another translation says, *"When people do not accept divine guidance, they run wild"* (NLT). *"If people can't see what God is doing, they stumble all over themselves"* (MSG).

The critical point is that a vision articulates a view of a realistic, credible, and attractive future for the organization, a condition that is better in some important ways than what now exists.
-Bennis and Nanus
Leaders: Strategies for Taking Charge

This image, which we call a vision, may be as vague as a dream or as precise as a goal or mission statement. To choose a direction, a leader must first have developed a mental image of a possible and desirable future state of the ministry. The critical point is that a vision articulates a view of a realistic, credible, and attractive future for the ministry.

93

"There is no more powerful engine driving an organization toward excellence and long-range success than an attractive, worthwhile, achievable vision for the future, widely shared."

—Burt Nanus

"A leader is one who sees more than others see, who sees farther than others see, and who sees before others do."

—Leroy Eims
Be the Leader You Were Meant to Be

"If you stay one step ahead of your people, you are called a leader. Stay ten steps ahead of your people, and you are called a martyr."

—Source unknown

"Vision for ministry is a clear mental image of a preferable future imparted by God to His chosen servants and is based upon an accurate understanding of God, self, and circumstances."

—George Barna

"A condition that is better in some important ways than what now exists. There is no more powerful engine driving an organization toward excellence and long-range success than an attractive, worthwhile, achievable vision for the future, widely shared."

—Burt Nanus 89

Most pastors lead by habit instead of vision. It was George Barna who said 95% of all pastors lead without vision. If that is true, then that only leaves 5% of pastors who have their ear to the voice of God for His divine purpose and plan for His church. My pastor once said, "If a man has a vision you can't stop him. If a man doesn't have a vision, you can't start him." It has been said that, "Vision is not a statement that is memorized; it is a move of God that is memorable."

It is of the utmost importance that pastors realize that they are responsible for the destiny of their members. Every pastor who has been given the trust by God to lead His people has a big responsibility to lead them to be the best they can be, not just in the best of times, but in the worst of times. We all can agree that this destiny has to do with our eternal destiny. Of course, that is the most important part of the call of every pastor. However, I also believe it has to do with the here and now.

As a pastor we must also be concerned and yes be involved in the lives of those we serve. Please don't misunderstand what I'm saying. I am not saying that the pastor should monopolize, control, or dominate the lives of those to whom they are called to serve. I believe that as the spiritual authority and representative for God as the pastor, the people that you serve should trust you enough to help them navigate the many challenges in this ever-changing, chaotic world. This means that those who the pastor serves as the servant leader, should be willing to submit to the spiritual leadership of the pastor. The Word of God instructs us to; *"Obey them that have the rule over you, and submit yourselves: for they watch for your souls, as they that must give account, that they may do it with joy, and not with grief: for that is unprofitable for you"* (Hebrews 13:17 KJV).

Another translation says it like this: *"Obey your spiritual leaders and do what they say. Their work is to watch over your souls, and they are accountable to God. Give them a reason to do this with joy and not with sorrow. That would certainly not be for your benefit"* (NLT).

Wow! What a great responsibility, watching over your souls. That's nothing to play around with, and besides that, God made the pastor responsible. Every pastor will have to give account to God who has placed people under him/her to serve them. Pastors are indeed responsible for the destiny of those they serve. Members are responsible for the vision of the pastor! The pastor's responsibility is to equip God's people to do His work and build up the church, the body of Christ. *"This will continue until we all come to such unity in our faith and knowledge of God's Son that we will be mature in the Lord, measuring up to the full and complete standard of Christ"* (Ephesians 4:12-13 NLT).

Every member of the church should recognize that they have a vital part to play in the vision of the church. While it is true that the pastor is the one who casts the vision for the ministry, it is also true that the members must take hold of that vision and work it until it comes to pass. If the church is not experiencing victory, it will be because of one or two things. *One*, the pastor has not cast a vision, and if so, maybe it's not clear. *Second,* it could be that the people refuse to run with it. If such is the case in either way, victory and fulfillment of the vision will not be manifested. If that happens, then the Lord will get no glory and the church will suffer.

CHAPTER 8
FIVE Ps FOR
CHANGE

1. Potential for Change

Philippians 4:13: *"I can do all things through Christ who strengthens me."*

Let me first say, don't ever let anyone tell you that you don't have what it takes to navigate seasons of change in your life. It is God who lives in you both to will and to do according to His will and good pleasure in you. The Lord has gifted us with the ability to do great things for His glory. Don't allow the enemy or anyone else to convince you of what can't be done when you have so much potential locked up on the inside just waiting to be released.

Every person born into this world is born with the potential to be and do something great for self, humanity, and God. God placed in us his *DNA*.

DNA, short for Deoxyribonucleic Acid, is an extremely long chain of molecules that contains all the information necessary for the life functions of a cell. The individual molecules that make up DNA are called nucleotides.

DNA is a self-replicating material that is present in nearly all living organisms as the main constituent of chromosomes. It is the carrier of genetic information. It is the fundamental and distinctive characteristics or qualities of someone or something, especially when regarded as unchangeable.

Don't worry, I will not bore you with all the scientific definitions, terms, or meanings of DNA. I only bring it to your attention to prove that before scientists ever discovered DNA, God had already invented it. It all started with Him. God was very creative in inventing cells, blood vessels, veins, fingerprints, hair particles, saliva, and anything else that is used to get the identity of a person. God was so detailed in His creation that no other person has your DNA. That's because you are made in His image and likeness.

Then God said, *"Let Us make man in Our image, after Our likeness! Let them rule over the fish of the sea, over the flying creatures of the sky, over the livestock, over the whole earth, and over every crawling creature that crawls on the land." God created humankind in His image, in the image of God He created him, male and female He created them* (Genesis 1:26 -27 TLV).

We are in fact created in His image and likeness. We have His distinctive characteristics and qualities of Him who is unchangeable, God. His image is the reflection of who we see when we look at ourselves in a mirror. Oh, we may have different skin, hair and eye color but beneath the skin, we are all the same. Likeness has to do with character. The ability to choose to do what is morally and ethically right and good. Coupled with this image and likeness is this thing we call **creation.** We, by nature, have the ability to create things, just as

God has and still does today. The sad fact is that satan introduced his will into the affairs of God in the Garden, and Adam forfeited much of the privileges given to us by choosing to willfully disobey God. However, that still did not cause God to withdraw man's ability to not experience God's image, likeness, or creating ability.

Because we were created by God, in His image and likeness, we have the potential to do great things—things that are only limited by the limitation that we place on our ability to create.

In his book, *Understanding Your Potential,* the late Dr. Miles Monroe states that God had revealed to him the true nature of potential and that he received a burden to teach others how to tap into their own God-given potential. According to Dr. Monroe, there are several questions that we must answer if we are going to ever fulfill God's purpose of having an effective life.

1. Who am I?
2. Why am I here?
3. What am I capable of doing?
4. What are my limitations?
5. Who sets the standards?

How you answer these questions will have a profound effect on what you accomplish in life and for God's Kingdom.

So, what is the thing we call potential and what's the big deal about it? Many people go through life empty and unfulfilled, never realizing nor living up to their

God-given potential. It is said that we use less than 10% of our potential, the other 90% goes unused, undeveloped, and unrealized.

One of the greatest tragedies in life is to allow potential to go to the grave undiscovered and untapped. Many people have died never realizing their potential because they did not understand the nature or concept of what potential is.

I remember as a child hearing the story of "The Little Engine That Could." I recall the famous quote, "I think I can... I think I can... I think I can." These words are repeated over and over again by the little blue engine as it pulls a train filled with toys over a mountain to a town to little children who have been good.

Three other trains decided not to go because of the difficult terrain to get to the town. Only the little engine was willing to try and, while repeating over and over again, "I think I can, I think I can," overcame the seemingly impossible task. The potential to change things is telling yourself, "I think I can . . . I think I can," when things look and even seem impossible.

There may be many other reasons not to make the decision to navigate difficult terrain in your personal life, business, relationships, and, yes, even ministry. If such is the case, make up your mind to look past every place that seems impossible and trust the One who created you and gifted you with the power to believe when believing is hard.

"Our life is a constant journey, from birth to death. The landscape changes, the people change, our needs change, but the train keeps moving. Life is the train, not the station."

—Paulo Coelho

There is a wealth of potential in every one of us. This is true because God placed it there. Be all that God has created you to be. You have the potential.

"Everyone has inside himself a piece of good news! The good news is that you really don't know how great you can be, how much you can love, what you can accomplish, and what your potential is!"

—Anne Frank

Potential is having or showing the capacity to become or develop into something in the future. It is defined as possible when the necessary conditions exist. It is latent qualities or abilities that may be developed and lead to future success or usefulness.

-https://dictionary.cambridge.org/
dictionary/english/potential

"The greatest waste in the world is the difference between what we are and what we could become."

—Dr. Ben Herbster

"Wealth, notoriety, place, and power are no measure of success whatsoever. The only true measure of success is the ratio between what we might have done and what we might have been on the one hand, and the thing we have made of ourselves on the other."

—H.G. Wells

2. <u>Purpose</u> for Change:

Romans 8:28: *"Now we know that all things work together for good for those who love God, who are called according to His purpose"* (TLV).

The purpose for change doesn't just happen. It takes making a decision to choose to do what is good and what is God's will for you and all those involved. It may not be popular or even culturally correct. What matters more than anything else is knowing you are doing what God created you to do. Dr. Miles Monroe once said, "To discover the purpose of something, never ask the creation; ask the creator." Our own ideas about our purpose are flawed and limited. We can find our true purpose only in the One who created us. Only He, God, knows the thoughts and plans He has for us. May I say they are good plans and have a good purpose? Purpose is what we were created for. It is the reason why we exist. Since such is the case, one would think that in order to fulfill true purpose, it would seem smart to talk to God.

Every plan, goal, and aspiration in life should have God's input.

The Bible lets us know, *"A man's heart plans his way, but the Lord directs his steps."* (Proverbs 16:9 NKJV).

Well, what exactly is this thing we call purpose? *Purpose* is defined as "The reason for which something exists or is done, made, used, etc." (Cambridge Dictionary). What must be understood is, if success is to be achieved, we must do everything in our power to know and understand the purpose. Only then can we really know what it means to live on purpose. Living on purpose will not just happen, it will require intentionality and steadfastness. Many challenges will come to distract and discourage you, which could take your focus.

Have you ever experienced a season in your life when things just didn't seem to go as you planned? You knew you were in the right place, doing all the right things, but it seemed like nothing was adding up. Nothing was working the way you imagined. Well, I have been there. Let me tell you, it's no fun. As a matter of fact, it was very frustrating, especially when you know you are moving with purpose, yet all you get is frustration. I call that "frustrated purpose." Now if you have never experienced seasons of frustration, just keep living, keep serving, and keep leading. Every one of these areas is purposeful, yet sometimes that leads to frustration.

Here's what I know when that happens, we must always go back to the One who created and gave us the reason why we exist and the reason that what we do matters. Here is what must be remembered, God created us with His purpose in mind. He said: "*I know the plans I have for you . . . plans to prosper you and not to harm you*" (NIV). We must resist the idea of planning without Him. God has a sense of humor. You don't believe it? Well then, tell God your plans and watch Him laugh. He has plans! So, let us acknowledge Him in all our ways and He will bring our true purpose to pass.

3. <u>Prepare</u> People for Change

God's purpose involves people. Face it! We are in the people business. As change agents, we must embrace the assignment of helping people live and become all that God intended for them to be. God is concerned about people and because He is, then we should be as well. Now you need to know that working with people can be a little messy sometimes. The challenge of preparing people for change is one that requires prayer, patience, and commitment. Ask pastor Moses, surely, he can tell you all about it. It has been said that basically there are three kinds of people in the world—people who are workers, people who are watchers, and people who are wonderers.

People who are workers are the ones who "make things happen. "These are people who need little to no motivation or encouragement. They are self-starters, independent workers, movers, and shakers. They simply know how to make things happen. You can give them an assignment and they will grab it like a hungry beast and will not turn loose until they have produced something with it. These are the people you want on your leadership team in your church. They just make great leaders. These are the people I call "change agents." The truth of the matter is, there are not many of this kind of people in the church.

The second kind of people in the world are known as those who sit back and "watch things happen." These types of people are just involved, but lack real commitment. I tell a story of the chicken and pig sometimes so people can really see the difference between true commitment and mere involvement. The story goes like this: "Who likes sausage or ham and egg biscuit for breakfast raise your hand? Most of the time everyone's hands go up. I proceed to say, there were two animals that participated in making it happen for you to enjoy that delicious sausage or ham and egg biscuit.

One of the animals was committed and the other was simply involved. The pig who was committed had to die. The chicken who was just involved dropped that egg and went on her way to lay an egg again another day. *The moral of the story is, Commitment will cost you your life, involvement costs you nothing.* People who sit back and watch things happen are not committed people, they are just involved. When and if they show up, they will stand around and just look. If they happen to get involved, it will not be because they initiated it, but because they were asked. When they do, there will be little or no real commitment. The sad fact is some of the members of the churches today fill this role.

Then there's the final classification of people— those who are clueless. When and if they show up, they "wonder what happened." They have no idea what is going on. They haven't paid any attention to the announcements, bulletins, or advertisements. They are completely lost. They will not volunteer, and if they do, they won't show up. You can't put any trust or stock in them. The sad fact is many of these are members of our churches today. As the pastor or leader, you have the responsibility of developing these types of people into productive members of the church. Remember, I said that the culture of the church is set by the pastor or leader. It all starts with you! You have the potential; you know and understand your purpose and now you must help the people know and understand their purpose.

First, let me challenge you to change the way you think about your assignment. See yourself as a change agent for God. After all; these are His people, and He has a purpose and plan for them. Yes, all of them! Don't allow the enemy to fill your mind with all the negative things that may or may not be happening in your church. I am not saying to simply ignore them. What I am saying is don't get so frustrated by them that you can't see the big picture. See the possibilities. Ask God to fix your thinking. Ask Him to give you the vision and true purpose for you, and the people you serve. When he does write it, share it and work on it. Change the way you view what you do. Understand that you have been called to an "apostolic assignment and not just a position." God has called, appointed, and anointed you for this good work.

A good way to begin would be to seek Him first and then start speaking positively over those you serve. Encourage instead of discouraging them. Train, preach and teach with transformational living in mind. Get excited about what God can do. Transformed by the renewing of your mind.

Stinking Thinking: negative thinking vs positive thinking.

I'll say more about what that looks like in "embracing the process."

4. Embrace the <u>Process</u> of Change:

Now that you know that you have the **potential** for change and you understand the true **purpose** of change and the people are **prepared** to change, let's talk about how to embrace the **process** of change. Process is a systematic series of actions directed to some end. It is a procedure or something you do in order to achieve a certain result. A process of change is needed to assist with guiding people and ministry to a positive desired state of growth and wellness. This is especially crucial in areas where ministry is in stagnation and decline.

You may recall me saying to the church that I served as pastor these words; "Change can be difficult, but change is necessary for survival." Change can be scary, uncertain, unpredictable, and uncomfortable. However, change must take place. God never said it would be easy, but what He did say is, that He would never leave nor forsake us.

Change is a process. This process must start with an evaluation of your current condition. An accurate written assessment of your current ministry state should include but not be limited to the following. The mission, vision, goals, and core values of the ministry. Mission speaks of who you are, vision speaks of what you want to do, goals are a systematic written plan of how you are going to do it and core values speak to what you believe or your non-negotiables.

Next an assessment of the various ministries that will be provided based on your mission, and vision.

Next, will be the people who will serve in the ministry. This will include any paid staff and volunteer positions.

Then there is the type of facilities that will house the ministry if needed. This will include the needed worship space, nursery/children's space, any classrooms, and office space.

Finally, a projected operations budget will need to be put together.

Once all this has been done then it should be committed to God in prayer for His blessings and guidance. After all, vision comes from God. Now you write the vision.

A well-written and articulated vision is the key to accomplishing what God has given to you and the church. It would also be a good idea to share it with key leaders who will also commit it to prayer. Once you have done that, it's time to share the vision with the entire church. I might add that preaching a sermon series leading up to a big vision casting event would be good. This will help the people to walk the journey with you over several weeks and then come to the final product of what God has given to the church.

I must add here, be ready for some pushback. There may be a few or some who may not be able to see where God is taking the church. Everybody may not see it all at once or in the same way. Some may never see it, so don't let the blindness of a few stop the blessings of the masses. Remember, don't allow yourself to become negative. Continue to share the vision, eventually they will come on board.

5. Experience the <u>Product</u> Through Change: Total Victory

Change will never happen if you don't make up your mind to change. After making up your mind you must remain consistent in the process. The word of God tells us that man with a double mind is unstable in all his ways. There will be days when it will seem like you can't kill nothing and nothing won't die. When that happens just remain steadfast to your potential, purpose, and process. The Lord will perform what He promised you. That's the product. Product represents victory here in the final phase of change.

What actually is this thing we call, product? A product is a thing or person that is the result of an action or process. It is what happens when everything is working the way it's designed to work with successful or greater outcomes. Sometimes in order for that to happen changes may need to take place. Regardless of how small, difficult, or scary, change has to happen before the product (victory) can be experienced.

CHAPTER 9
SUCCESSFUL
RELAUNCH CHANGE

Change can be measured in terms of success only after fruitful progress. When change is experienced, newness, freshness, and increase happen. There is a sense of accomplishment and satisfaction from all people involved.

I shared with you in the previous chapter some basic questions the Lord asked me during my season of frustration. Those questions were first posed to me personally. I was experiencing a season of stagnation within myself which led to a season of frustration within the ministry. After God rebuked me, He then directed my attention to the church. I cannot tell you how liberating this revelation was to me. You see, after placing the blame at my feet, and I accepted responsibility for my personal condition, I was able to clearly see and cast a new vision for the church. I returned home from my meeting in Cleveland, Tennessee, and pulled together what I called our new Ministry Assimilation Team. I shared the vision with the team, and we began the process of strategic planning to relaunch the ministry. It all started with changing our emphasis from church membership to having people connect and experience a journey with the ministry.

The process included revisiting our mission, vision statement, and motto. All of this had to line up with our core values. One of our biggest emphases was moving people from one stage to the next in their personal, spiritual, and ministry journey with the Lord and the church. This was an intentional process that fostered growth tracks for our current members, as well as those whom the Lord would send us. Our planning also included new branding and a massive marketing campaign to get the word out about who we were, what we did, why we did it, and what we hoped to gain from doing it. Here is what our vision assimilation process looked like.

In order for change to take place, it was imperative that a new well-thought-out mission and vision statement be developed. For us, it was simple. We looked at who we were, what our true purpose was, and then what we wanted to accomplish. First and foremost, we settled the fact that we are a church, and I might add not just any church. We reaffirmed that we are a Pentecostal, Bible believing, Bible preaching, Bible teaching, Spirit-led, life-transforming church. So, it made sense that our mission should line up with who we are.

We then proceeded to get our new mission statement from the Bible, which happens to have the greatest mission statement of all times. It was clear to me that the Gospel of Matthew, Chapter 28, which contains the Great Commission, recorded the words of our Lord Jesus to His disciples, and now to us. So, we chose one word, "GO" as our mission. I'm amazed at how we want people to come to our church, when we never go out to where they are. In other words, *we have a "go-to gospel with a come-to mentality."* The mission of the church at its core is to go into the hedges and highways and compel men, women, boys and girls to come to Jesus. So here is what our vision casting for change looked like.

Our scripture text that defined the mission was . . . *"Go ye therefore and teach all nations, baptizing them in the name of the Father, and of the Son, and of the Holy Ghost; teaching them to observe all things whatsoever I have commanded you. And lo I am with you always, even unto the end of the world. Amen"* (Matthew 28:19-20 KJ21). We then decided what would be the outcome once we accomplished our mission to "Go." From that, we came up with a simple **Vision Statement**. Our new vision statement was, **"Transformed Lives, Transformed Church, Transformed Community."** If we really wanted people to experience genuine faith in Jesus which led to conversion and discipleship, it had to be intentional. Once individuals were transformed then the corporate church would experience transformation. Once the corporate church experienced life-giving life-sustaining change, we would be ready to engage our community.

Several questions that surfaced in our discussion were: How do we do community-based ministry? What would it look like? What makes our church different from any other church in our community? Why would people attend here? All these questions are good and need answers. However, the most important question that came up, was: "If our church doors closed today would the community miss it?" The sad fact is that many churches could close today, and the community would never miss it. Could it be that the church spends most of their time focusing on what's happening within the four walls instead of what's happening all around it in the community. We decided to shift some of our attention into marketplace ministry, the community, and the city where we were. This became a major part of our assimilation process.

Our **Vision Scripture** text we selected for the church was . . . *"We all, with unveiled face, beholding as in a mirror the glory of the Lord, are being transformed into the same image from glory to glory, just as by the Spirit of the Lord"* (2 Corinthians: 3:18 NKJV).

From there we came up with our **Ministry Motto:** *"We're here for you. Connect and Experience the Journey!"* We wanted those we connected with to know that our whole purpose for being a church was to make them feel that we saw them and that they mattered. After all, if they mattered to God then they should matter to us. I remember someone saying to me years ago, "People don't care how much you know until they know how much you care!" The church of Jesus Christ must demonstrate love above all else if she expects hurting, lost, and disenfranchised people to connect with her.

After formulating our **mission, vision,** and **motto,** we began the process of developing key aspects of the direction of the ministry and what we would accomplish. We started by answering the question: Who Are WE?

It was at this junction that I realized many of the members of the church really did not know who we, as a church, were. I remember God asking me that very same question, and I did just like those I asked about the church. Their response was just like my response. They began to tell me what we did—things like, we pray, study the Word of God, worship the Lord, preach, sing, and the list goes on.

So, our first job would be to define who we are as a church. Much of what we came up with was based on short statements that the members would have no problem remembering and sharing when asked the question in the community. Here is what we came up with. We are….

1. **God Inspired:** A God-breathed genuine ministry, led by the power of the Holy Spirit.
2. **Christ Centered:** A life-changing relationship with Christ as Lord, Savior, and Master.
3. **Family Focused:** A family emphasis within the church and community.

We believe these three were the basis of what ministry should be all about. A great deal of time was invested in developing each of them to include preaching a series of sermons, teaching sessions, printed materials, and marketing within the church. Everything we did was based on our being God Inspired, Christ Centered, and Family Focused. This is who we are. The very next phase had to do with: What Do We Do?

The church adopted what we refer to as an *"assimilation process."* This process consisted of *five phases* to move people from one stage to another on their personal, family, and spiritual journey. Each phase was designed to provide guidance toward personal and corporate life transformation as a mature disciple of Christ. Each of the five-step processes had the caveat of connecting behind it.

Five Phases of Our Assimilation Process:

A. Evangelism Connection: We believe that the foundation of all ministries starts with *evangelism.* The witnessing and saving of souls are what ministry is all about. If a church focus is not on souls being saved and added to the kingdom of God, it should close its doors.

How we did it:
- **Witnessing:** One-on-one and group-sharing personal testimony
- **Salvation:** Sharing the good news of Jesus Christ
- **Community Outreach:** Organizing and promoting various community events

B. Discipleship Connection: Our next step in the assimilation process was *discipleship.* It's not enough to get people to come to the saving grace of Jesus. After they accept Him, they need to know how to live for Him. They also need to know what it means to let the light of Christ shine through them so that others will see their good works and God get the glory. Discipleship, in its simplest definition, is "The process of teaching and following the doctrines and precepts of Christ."

118

How we did it:

- **New Disciples Classes:** Teaching new converts how to live the life of Christ.
- **New Members Classes:** Teaching new members through connect classes.
- **Sunday School:** Teaching age-appropriate classes on faith and foundation of the Bible.
- **Bible Study:** Systematically studying the Bible for personal and corporate growth.
- **Christian Education:** Christian formation and transformation teaching.

C. Ministry Connection: The next step in our process was called *"ministry connect."* This step is vital as it spoke of working in the ministry after connecting with the church. It only seems logical that saved, discipled, new members, should be involved in some ministry assignment within the church. Members who are serious and committed about their faith and love their church will be eager to get involved in the ministry. We used a ministry-gifting assessment prior to placing anyone in any particular ministry assignment. The days of plug and play are over. A gift assessment helps to place people in places where they are gifted and enjoy working. When that happens, ministry is emphasized, not a job or duty assignment.

How we did it:

- Men's Ministry
- Women's Ministry
- Youth and Discipleship Ministry
- Children's and Student Ministry

- Ministry of Helps
- Music Ministries
- Young at Heart Ministry (single adult)

D. Life Connections: Our next stage in the assimilation process was our *life connect.* We realized that people on average spent somewhere between 3 to 5 hours a week in a corporate worship experience. The rest of that time was spent doing what we call life. So, it made sense to us that if people spent more of their time doing life, maybe we needed to help them navigate ways to help them be successful, especially from a Biblical perspective. So, we started life-connect groups within the church. Now, we did not just place anybody over them; we made sure the leaders were committed and faithful to the church. Connecting people and families to life-giving groups and in things that they love doing will grow your church faster than anything else.

How we did it:
- Life Group
- Singles and Soaring
- Unity Team: Unfolding, New, Ideals, Together with You
- Sports

E. Leadership Connection: The final step in our process was *leadership connect.* This stage was the one that I led. One of our policies was that in order for a member to be elevated into leadership, the member would have to go through all the previous stages. To serve in leadership required a commitment level far above any other stage in our process. It also was not something that just happened overnight.

How we did it:
Leadership advancement is achieved by undergoing training and development in various official capacities as outlined within the ministry structure.

- Lay Leadership: training and development of lay leaders in ministry
- Elders/Deacons
- Ministry Leaders
- Church Mothers
- Reverends: Credentialed ministers within the body

After meeting, planning, and strategizing for about six months with the assimilation team, we were ready to present the vision to the church. Each member of the assimilation team was responsible for developing a plan which included any assistance needed by other members of the team, or members of the church, and promotional materials. I will go ahead and admit here that I wanted them to do a dry run first of what they would be sharing with the corporate church. Of course, that was met with resistance. They had the nerve to tell me, "We've been in training with you for over six months, we know what you expect, we know what to do and if we show it to you first, you will make changes." Where they got me is when they said to me, "You are just going to have to trust us with this." We want you to see it when everyone else sees it.

Now for those who know me, you are probably wondering what I did. Well, let me just say that I got my first viewing at the same time as the church did. I would admit, I was a little nervous because I had no idea what to expect. However, I trusted them because I poured into them what the Lord poured into me. On the weekend prior to our new relaunch service, they decorated the entire church with balloons, ribbons, and streamers. All throughout the church classrooms, in the front lobby, down the hallways, and in the fellowship hall, sign-up booths were set up for members to connect, get information, and to participate in our new ministry opportunities within the church.

A massive marketing campaign had been carried out all month long, leading up to the grand relaunch day. When Sunday morning came, we were met with new T-shirts that had our new brand on them. Everyone was excited, and in expectation of the new relaunch. All throughout the church, people were laughing, fellowshipping, taking pictures at photo booths, or just in front of decorations.

Then the time came for us to enter the sanctuary for the main event—the new relaunch of our church, **Cornerstone Family Worship Center.** When Lisa and I walked in, we were greeted with loud worship music playing over the sound system and people shouting and giving God the praise. This Sunday morning was not like any other we've experienced ever before. I would not sit in my usual seat designated for the pastor, this morning we were just one of the members waiting to see what all the talk and excitement was about. Again, those of you who know me, you know that Sunday morning was about Kingdom business. I mean, the worship team would get up and sing a few songs to open the service, someone would do the devotional, someone else would come receive the tithes and offerings, and the worship team would sing one last song before I would come and preach. After preaching, I would make my altar appeal, pray for the people, then we would fellowship a bit, and then go home. Sunday morning was strictly business for me. Now don't get it twisted, we had church. Does this sound like anyone you know?

Well, on this relaunch Sunday morning, I was not the center of attention. The pulpit would not be filled by me, at least not by myself, and certainly not first. With excitement and cheers filling the sanctuary the first person to take the stage was Sarah Godley, our new Evangelism Connect Team Coordinator. She presented her evangelism emphasis on PowerPoint with enthusiasm and excitement, and blew it out of the water.

Next was Elder Shirley Roberson, our new Discipleship Connect Team Coordinator. She presented her PowerPoint presentation on the process of discipleship and the steps to become a disciple of Jesus Christ. She too blew it out of the water.

Behind her came Joshua and Sabre McIntyre, our new Ministry Connect Team Coordinators. They shared their PowerPoint presentation on the various ministry opportunities offered by the church and what it took to connect and experience the journey with us. They blew it out of the water.

They were followed by Rob and Latrice Peele who were our new Life Connect Ministry Coordinators. They presented their PowerPoint presentation on how to connect with life groups and do ministry within and outside the church. They blew it out of the water.

Finally, it was my time. I don't mind telling you now that I felt a little intimidated. I mean those who came before far surpassed my expectations. It was evident by the reception they received by the church that morning. Now it was my time to share my presentation on how to connect with the church in leadership. I shared my PowerPoint and explained our process which included all of the other connect phases, finally getting a person to leadership in the church. After I finished, the congregation was encouraged to take an active part in their church by going to visit each of the connect booths that were set up all around the church. There, they would receive information about the church and all the ministry opportunities available in which they could participate.

The morning concluded with refreshments in the fellowship hall, excitement of laughter, picture taking, and having good fellowship. I remember saying to myself: Now my church has a better idea and can share with those they come in contact with, who we are, what we do, why we do it, and what we hope to gain from doing it.

When was the last time you revisited your vision, mission, and core values of your church? If you asked your members who the church is, what it did, and what the purpose was for doing it, could they tell you? Does your church have an assimilation process to move people from salvation to becoming an active, contributing member? What about the community, do they know your church exists? If your church doors closed today, would your community miss it?

CHAPTER 10
MAINTAINING
SUCCESSFUL
CHANGE

In the business world, productivity and success are measured by evaluating the systems, procedurals, and practices for continued growth. Some companies use specific data to measure success. It goes without saying, but I will say it anyway: Success and productivity will not just happen automatically, neither will it continue to happen. You must take an active role in making sure continued progress is taking place. Rest assured, the longer you do a thing the more comfortable you will become with it. When this happens, corners are cut, concessions are made, and quality is sacrificed. It happens in our personal lives, workplace, relationships, and especially in our ministry assignments. We must give the strictest care to guarding what God has invested in us.

Remember, the culture of the church is set by the leader, so what you expect, you should be inspecting on a consistent basis. This should be done in your personal life and ministry, for the entire corporate church, and in every ministry department within the church. The measuring stick outlined within this book is the heartbeat for who you are, why you do what you do, and what you hope to gain from doing it.

Let's explore three areas that should be evaluated for maintaining constant success: *Personal, Corporate Church, and Ministry Departments within the church.*

1. Personal: This has to do with you the pastor, leader, the one calling the shots, the one God has anointed and appointed over His church.

Once you have accomplished your desired change of success, you must commit to a systematic process of spiritual discipline of daily devotions, of prayer, and scripture intake, to maintain freshness, and stay in tune with what the Lord is saying, and doing. I know this is not always easy, because there will always be something or somebody that will demand your attention and time. Remember, I know because I pastored, so what I'm saying is not something somebody told me. I have been there, and I feel for you. Let me encourage you to do your very best to put yourself in check, because if not, then, the Lord certainly will! Continued self-evaluation and inspection should be the order of the day.

Dr. Fred Garmon, founder and facilitator of LeaderLabs, in his book; *Ten Essential Skills, Executive Leadership Program,* says; "The absolute number one prerequisite for leadership is learning enough about yourself to lead others."

2. Corporate Church: The next area that should be evaluated should be your place of service. Dr. Garmon's, *Ten Essential Skills of Leadership*, also said: "Feedback is a gift."

Whether you work a job, or are in a ministry assignment, evaluation should be done on the staff, facilities, property, operations, maintenance, fiscal management, and anything else that oversight should be given. I want to speak specifically to pastors here. As the pastor of Cornerstone, I realized that my responsibility in the ministry was not just to the Sunday morning worship experience. I was just as responsible for my office staff, the fiscal management, property, and facilities. We had those who made sure these things were taken care of, and I'm so grateful we did. However, at the end of the day, I still had general oversight because I was the pastor. The truth is that every one of these areas played a part in the vision and success of the ministry. One of the things that helped in my pastorate was allowing my congregation to survey me as the pastor and spiritual leader of the church.

Once a year I would provide a survey with a small comment section at the end for those who felt the need to express something they believed I needed to know. All right, I see smoke coming from your ears. You are probably thinking, man you must be crazy. You, allowed your church to evaluate you. Yes, I did. I was evaluating them, so why not let them evaluate me? The purpose was to highlight blind spots in my pastoral and ministry skills, so I could address them for personal, and ministry growth for successful change. It was not designed to be used as an instrument to throw potshots at me or my ability to serve the congregation. However, you know as well as I do, there is always someone that will take their liberty to do so. However, I found the survey to be useful.

You see, I realized early in my ministry that people talked. Whether you want to admit it or not, it's true. On Sunday morning, right after the morning service, some of your members will come right up to you, look you in the face, smile, and shake your hand like you are the best thing in the world to them. Some of those same people will go home and sit down around the dinner table and serve you up as the main course. Maybe you said or did something they didn't agree with, and they just felt the need to get it off their chest. I concluded that if people are going to serve me up, then at least I should know about it. After all, I'm the only one who can address and fix it.

No matter how good a job you are doing at your place of employment, or in your ministry assignment, there is always room for improvement. How will you ever know it unless, someone tells you. I want to know. So, I created a survey and allowed those whom I served to evaluate me. It was a tool that was used to provide feedback to help improve me and the ministry. For me, it was asking the people I served. Their responses were provided on a sliding scale from 1—poor, 2—fair, 3—average, 4— good, 5—very good. This scale was used to rate my vision casting, vision implication, preaching and teaching, leadership skills, communication skills, dress, my ability to be able to relate well with others, and some more areas. I even had a couple of questions that pertained to how people saw me in the community and in the church. Since this was feedback about me, I was the only person who saw and read them. I read every comment both good and bad. Yes, there were a few bad ones, but I didn't let them discourage me. Most of the time, I knew who the people were who made them. I could tell if they had an axe to grind or if they genuinely wanted to help me see potential blind spots in my leadership. Not one time did I ever try to get back at those who tried to take advantage of the opportunity to vent. When I finished reading the evaluations, I shredded and trashed them.

3. Ministry Departments and Staff: I used the same process for evaluating the ministry.

Success and growth personally and ministerially are not something that just happens automatically. It takes time and intentionality on everyone's part. Maintaining a successful ministry will require change and adjustments to be made. As I mentioned in a previous chapter, change is difficult, but change is necessary if growth is achieved. You have heard the old saying; "Insanity is doing the same thing over and over again, but expecting a different result." Remember, you have been called, you are appointed, and you are anointed, so go be a change agent.

NAVIGATE YOUR SEASONS OF CHANGE!

Navigating the Seasons of Change

Author Biography

Dr. James S. McIntyre, Sr. has served the Church of God as a lead pastor of Cornerstone Family Worship Center and District Overseer for the Pamlico District, Washington North Carolina for over 20 years. He has also served on various State, Regional and International Boards and Committees. He has served on the ENC State Council; Youth and Discipleship, USA Mission, Ministerial Internship Program, Church Plant/ Revitalization Boards.

He has served as a member of Home for Children's Board of Trustees Eastern North Carolina. Regionally, he served as the President of the Church of God Southeast Regional Fellowship (SERF). Internationally he has served as a member of Pathway Press Editorial and Publications Board of Trustees, USA Missions Board, Lee University Board of Directors and a member of the Black Ministries Committee Church of God, Cleveland TN.

Dr. McIntyre earned his undergraduate and Doctoral of Theology Degrees with a concentration in Marriage and Family Counseling from Christian Life School of Theology, Columbus GA. He has earned various certifications in Certificate In Ministerial Studies (CIMS) with concentrations in Biblical, Pastoral and Doctrinal Studies from the Church of God Division of Education; Certifications in Excellence In Covenant Leadership, from the Pentecostal Theological Seminary; Certifications of Level's I & II Community Service

Chaplain and Certifications as a Trainer in the Ten Essential Skills of Executive Leadership from Leader Labs Inc, Cleveland TN.

He is married to Lady Lisa McIntyre for over 40 years. To this holy union, God has birth three sons, James Jr. Jonathan, and Joshua. They are also blessed with one daughter-in-love, Sabre and four grandchildren, Jayden, Jirah, Averie Grace and James Douglas.